Cake Decorating
with
Modeling Chocolate

Kristen Coniaris

BUTTERCREAM PRESS
CAMBRIDGE, MA

Copyright © 2013 Kristen Coniaris

Book 1 in the Wicked Goodies Series

Published by Buttercream Press
www.ButtercreamPress.com
Book Shepherd: Judith Briles
Cover and text design: Rebecca Finkel, F + P Graphic Design
Editor: Mira Perrizo

9   8   7   6   5   4   3   2

978-0-9886454-0-0 print
978-0-9886454-1-7 ebook

Library of Congress Cataloging-in-Publication 2012922561

Printed by Four Colour Print Group in South Korea

Since the turn of the century, amateur and professional bakers have frosted cakes with a newfangled icing called fondant that is like play dough. As a pastry chef, I've worked with commercial fondant extensively and appreciate its forgivingness and usability. However I am not a big fan of the gummy mouth feel, starchy flavor, and dubious fact that *technically* you can eat it but probably you shouldn't.

In 2008, I learned the art of modeling chocolate while freelancing as a 3D cake sculptor/decorator at *Cake*, a boutique bakery where "rolled chocolate" is used to form exquisite bows, ribbons, roses, and wraps for upscale wedding and specialty cakes. It is *delectable* stuff that is extremely easy to make and eats like candy. I was instantly hooked.

In 2010, I launched Wicked Goodies, which at the time was a custom cake operation. That year, I decorated all of my wedding and party cake designs with modeling chocolate using techniques that I had learned from other bakers, read about, or innovated myself. Meanwhile, I photographed the working process of every cake that I sold, which is how the material for this book came into existence. Now I am pleased to present the results of that dessert adventure, the very first full-length book on the topic, *Cake Decorating with Modeling Chocolate*. Please join me now in spreading the good word about this awesome confection.

—KRISTEN CONIARIS
Creator of Wicked Goodies

Contents

 49

 82

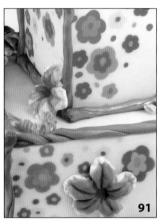 91

 94

 97

65

68

70

74

77

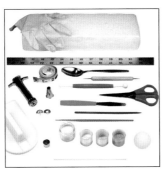

54

61

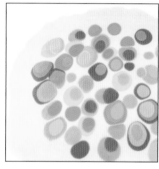
121

126

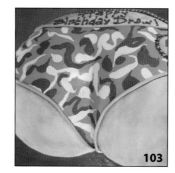

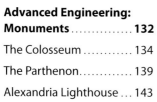

Introduction

All of the content herein was generated by **Wicked Goodies** between 2010–2011 with the exception of one cake that I made as a freelance cake artist for another bakery. Most of the cakes sold for somewhere between $70–$800. Much thanks to the clients whose unique visions helped shape the direction of this book, especially Yanni Alexander Shainsky and Victoria Leonidova-Shtilkiny, Josh and Heather Vaughn, Irina Poliak and Gil Gonzalez, Vincene and Walter Fix, Cynthia Hallowatch, Ron and Valerie Rivera, David Nolan, and Christy Thompson.

Thanks to the talented chefs whose experience and knowledge contributed to this material, especially Jennifer David Duncan and Esther Lee. Thanks to my West Coast family: Erica and Franco, Larisse and Charles, Tara and Marc, Heidi, Scott, Ronna and Ricky for your support and friendship while Wicked Goodies operated in San Diego. Thanks to Julie Darling of Just Call Us Kitchen Rentals and to Olivewood Gardens for letting us film a TLC show all over the place. Thanks to Nina Feldman for your eagle eye and to Mira Perrizo for the fine tuning. Thanks to Rebecca Finkel for devising the layout and to Judith Briles, The Book Shepherd for seeing this project through to completion. Thanks and love to Mike for believing in me. Thank you to Morgen Van Vorst and Rachel Dewoskin for teaching me about writing and encouraging me to pursue this goal. Thanks, above all, to my mom for a lifetime of baking inspiration.

Note All mm and cm conversions used in this book have been rounded to the nearest whole number.

Modeling Chocolate, also known as *plastic chocolate, chocolate leather,* or *candy clay,* is a soft, pliable confection made from chocolate and sugar syrup. It can be used in place of fondant for nearly every existing decorating technique. Although it requires more patience and finesse than fondant, it is far superior in flavor and versatility. Sweet and creamy, it melts on the tongue like soft, candy bar nougat. Slow to dry, it is the ideal substance for modeling shapes and figurines.

Rolled Modeling Chocolate is the term
for modeling chocolate that has been rolled by hand
or through a machine until thin. Rolled modeling
chocolate is an excellent medium for rendering
flower petals, leaves, ribbons, bows, and fabric effects. It can be used to wrap cakes as
an upscale alternative to fondant. It can be marbled or patterned with any design.

Ingredients

From scratch, modeling chocolate has only two ingredients: chocolate + sugar syrup. There is no tempering of chocolate involved; however, the technique and handling requires a similar level of care and understanding of chocolate. Note that the quality of modeling chocolate is only as delicious as the chocolate used to make it. Additionally, the proportion of sugar syrup to chocolate in the modeling chocolate formulas may require adjustments depending on the brand/quality of chocolate used.

Chocolate The Classifications of Chocolate and How They Pertain to Modeling Chocolate

• Bittersweet or Extra Dark Chocolate has the lowest percentage of sugar and therefore, the edgiest flavor. It is often denoted by the percentage of cocoa materials present, which can range anywhere from 35–100 percent. The higher the percentage of cocoa, the lower the percentage of sugar and the more bitter the taste. Bittersweet chocolate, rich in both color and taste, makes an excellent, not-too-sweet modeling chocolate.

• Semisweet or Dark Chocolate is typically intended for baking purposes and commonly found in chip form. It is essentially dark chocolate that has been sweetened at 1:2 ratio of sugar to cocoa. It works well for modeling chocolate.

• *Sweet Chocolate* is a term used only by U.S. standards to represent a lower quality sweetened chocolate containing no more than 15 percent real chocolate liquor. It works fine for modeling chocolate but has a diminished quality of taste.

• *Milk Chocolate* is dark chocolate with a milk product added. Although it can be used for modeling chocolate, its softness is not optimal for ease of handing or stability.

• *Compound Chocolate* is the technical term for imitation chocolate that is made with some or all hydrogenated fats in place of real cocoa butter. Compound chocolate can be used for modeling chocolate, but it may be less stable and less tasty. The formula requires 10–20 percent less sugar syrup.

• *White Chocolate,* a confection composed of sugar, milk and fat(s), is the basis of all colors of modeling chocolate except brown and black. True white chocolate contains cocoa butter, which lends an ivory tint to the hue. Imitation brands like Nestlé's (U.S.) Premium White Morsels and Merkens Super White Confectionery Coating substitute hydrogenated fats for cocoa butter.

Quality Comparison

Imitation White Chocolate

Sugar
Hydrogenated Oils
Dried Milk
Titanium Dioxide (whitener)
Artifical Flavors

Genuine White Chocolate

Sugar
Cocoa Butter
Dried Cream
Vanilla

Merkens
Super White Confectionery Coating

Nestlé (US)
Premium White Morsels

Callebut
White Bloc

Guittard
White Ripple Chunks

Resulting Modeling Chocolate Hues

Resulting Modeling Chocolate Properties

Made with Imitation White Chocolate	Made with Genuine White Chocolate
• Easier to achieve bright colors	• Difficult to achieve bright blues and purples
• Soft, sticky, marshmallowy consistency	• More elastic and durable
• Harder to handle with hot hands	• Easier to handle with hot hands
• Requires less corn syrup/glucose	• Requires more corn syrup/glucose

Sugar Syrup

Corn Syrup, or light corn syrup, is the optimal sugar syrup for modeling chocolate because of its pliability and resistance to crystallization. In the U.S., it is cheap and readily available. Outside the U.S., it is harder to find and may be prohibitively expensive. Unfortunately, its manufacturing process cannot be replicated in an ordinary home kitchen. Those who do not have access to corn syrup may opt to use liquid glucose instead.

Liquid Glucose, a slightly more dense sugar syrup, may be substituted for corn syrup. It is too complex to produce in the average home kitchen but it is obtainable worldwide. It tends to be costly.

Note: Corn syrup and liquid glucose are the most suitable sugar syrups for modeling chocolate. Golden syrup may be used but it will yellow the tone of white modeling chocolate significantly. Dark corn syrup may also be used but due to its brownish tone is only recommended for use in dark modeling chocolate. Substituting honey, agave, treacle, molasses, or simple syrup will result in a sticky mass. Therefore, it is not recommended.

Formulas

Bittersweet Modeling Chocolate

Bittersweet Chocolate	~2 cups*	12oz	340g
Corn Syrup or Glucose	½ cup or more	6 oz or more	174g (118ml) or more

Semisweet Modeling Chocolate

Semisweet Chocolate	~2 cups*	12oz	340g
Corn Syrup or Glucose	⅓ cup + 2T or more	5.7 oz or more	160g (108ml) or more

Milk Chocolate Modeling Chocolate

Mlk Chocolate	~2 cups*	12oz	340g
Corn Syrup or Glucose	⅓ cup + 1T or more	4.8 oz or more	139g (94ml) or more

White Chocolate Modeling Chocolate

White Chocolate	~2 cups*	12oz	340g
Corn Syrup or Glucose	⅓ cup or more	4.1 oz or more	116g (79ml) or more

*The volume of chocolate differs depending on the shape of the chunks/morsels used. Weighing the chocolate for this formula is highly recommended for the most accurate and consistent results.

Execution
Quick Microwave Method

Items Needed

- Microwave
- Chocolate + sugar syrup (see Formulas page 16)
- 1 medium-size glass or ceramic bowl, clean and dry
- 1 small microwave safe bowl for heating the sugar syrup
- Firm spatula (make at home by trimming the excess rubber off the edges of an ordinary spatula with a pair of scissors) or alternatively, a stainless steel spoon
- Plastic wrap
- Zipper-close freezer bag

1. Chop the chocolate, if necessary, and pour it into a clean, dry glass bowl.

2. Microwave the chocolate, uncovered, for 20–30 seconds on high (microwave times may vary). Remove the bowl from the microwave and mix the chocolate with a firm spatula or a spoon.

3. Repeat for another 15–20 seconds, stirring immediately afterwards. Continue with short bursts in the microwave followed by stirring until all the chocolate has melted and no hard bits remain. It is critical that the chocolate not be overheated at this point or it may seize (harden), or worse, scorch.

If the bottom of the bowl grows too hot to touch, the chocolate is in danger of overheating. If that is the case, stir well to redistribute the heat.

4. In a separate bowl, microwave the sugar syrup for 30 seconds or until warm. It must not be hot or it may burn the chocolate.

5. Pour the warm syrup over the chocolate and stir with the firm spatula until just blended. The chocolate will quickly stiffen. Here is white (below):

And here is dark (right), which at this stage tends to be looser than white modeling chocolate.

6. Pour the mixture onto a sheet of plastic wrap. Flatten it into a patty and seal it well. Rest it on a sheet pan or cool tabletop at room temperature for 1–3 hours or until it begins to resemble a soft Tootsie Roll in consistency. If the environment is warm, it may take up to 24 hours for a batch to set to a workable consistency. A fast set can be achieved by placing the wrapped chocolate in the refrigerator for half an hour, but a slow set at a cool room temperature yields the most stable product.

7. Once it is semi-firm, knead the modeling chocolate with the palm of the hand for 10–20 seconds or until smooth. Those with hot hands may opt to work the chocolate with a bench scraper instead.

8. Transfer the finished modeling chocolate to a heavy-duty, well-sealed bag for storage. Store it in a cool place out of sunlight. For long-term storage, keep sealed bags of rolled modeling chocolate in an airtight container away from heat and not in the refrigerator. Modeling chocolate can last for up to a year if stored properly.

Stovetop Method

Items Needed

- Chocolate + sugar syrup (see page 16 for Formulas)
- Medium-size glass or stainless steel bowl, clean and dry
- Medium-size saucepan filled with water 1-inch (25mm) deep for use as double boiler
- Firm spatula or alternatively, a stainless steel spoon
- Plastic wrap
- Zipper-close freezer bag

1. Chop the chocolate, if necessary, and pour it into a clean, dry glass bowl.

2. Set the bowl atop the saucepan to complete a double boiler. Do not allow the water to come in contact with the bottom of the bowl. Set the heat to low/simmer.

3. Melt the chocolate slowly over gentle steam-induced heat, stirring frequently with the firm spatula. Do not allow the chocolate to overheat or it may burn. Do not allow steam to escape near the chocolate as the moisture may cause the chocolate to seize.

4. Continue to stir until no lumps remain.

5. Remove the bowl from the double boiler and set it down on a dry kitchen towel.

6. Proceed to Step 4 of the Quick Microwave Method but heat the sugar syrup in a small saucepan instead.

Coloring

Modeling chocolate may be tinted any color. Water or gel-based food colorings are both suitable; there is no need to invest in more expensive candy coloring. Powdered colorings may be used, but should be saturated with a small amount of water first.

Stirring in Color

The easiest way to color modeling chocolate is to do so in the production phase by adding liquid food coloring along with the sugar syrup. No additional work is required with this method since the color blends in automatically during the stirring and kneading stages. How much coloring is required to achieve a particular hue depends largely on the strength of the dye. If color is added in high concentration (more than ¼ teaspoon of liquid color added per 16 oz [454 g] batch of modeling chocolate), the excess liquid may cause a batch to go soft. Dark red modeling chocolate, for example, requires so much food coloring that the sugar syrup should be reduced by a teaspoon or more to offset the added moisture.

Kneading in Color

Color may be kneaded by hand into finished modeling chocolate. This method is useful when only a small amount of any particular color is needed.

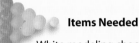

Items Needed

- White modeling chocolate
- 2 rubber gloves
- Liquid food coloring
- Cornstarch

1. Wearing rubber gloves to protect the skin from the dye, deposit a drop or more of food coloring onto a chunk of white modeling chocolate.

2. Add equal amounts of cornstarch as food coloring to help offset the added moisture and prevent stickiness.

3. Knead the food coloring and cornstarch into the modeling chocolate until thoroughly blended.

4. Add more color as needed until the desired hue is achieved. If a color ends up too dark in tone, add more white modeling chocolate to lighten the tone.

Note The mechanical action of kneading warms and softens modeling chocolate to the extent that it will require rest before it can be handled again. Therefore when kneading in color, plan to do so at least one hour in advance of rolling/modeling.

Whitening

The yellow tone of good quality white modeling chocolate can be so far from true white that achieving certain colors may pose a challenge; for instance, violet and light blue are impossible to attain in concert with yellow. Titanium dioxide, a natural white food coloring, may be added to whiten the base tone of modeling chocolate. For one batch of modeling chocolate, add ½ teaspoon of liquid titanium dioxide to the sugar syrup or ¼ teaspoon of powdered titanium dioxide dissolved in ½ teaspoon warm water. Alternatively, use a white chocolate that includes titanium dioxide in its ingredients.

Blackening

The color black is easiest to achieve by adding black food coloring to bittersweet modeling chocolate. Since bittersweet is quite dark to begin with, the least amount of coloring is required. Be sure to wear gloves when mixing black.

Bleeding

When a finished cake is exposed to temperature extremes, condensation may form on the surface, causing dark colors to bleed or streak. Tiers that have been decorated in modeling or rolled modeling chocolate should be sealed in plastic wrap to prevent sweat from beading on cake surfaces. A cake exposed to drastic temperature changes (going from fridge to room temperature, or the worst of all, freezer to room temperature) will develop condensation on its surface, which is not optimal for the appearance of rolled modeling chocolate.

In general, 3D decorations should be added to a cake at the last possible minute—dark-colored decorations in particular. As with fondant, the least amount of time a dark decoration comes in direct contact with the moist surface of a cake or a moist refrigerator climate, the more stable it will remain. Bows, flowers, and toppers are best transported to an event on parchment paper-lined sheet pans or in silicone molds, then added to the cake upon assembly.

For additional security, brush the back sides of dark decorations with melted cocoa butter. Allow the cocoa butter a minute or two to harden and seal before applying the decoration to the cake. The cocoa butter will serve as a buffer between opposing colors, minimizing streaking and bleeding.

Note Do not brush the front side of colored decorations with cocoa butter unless "frosty" is the desired effect.

Troubleshooting
Common Production Problems

Broken Emulsion

Invariably, some batches lose their emulsion or "break" which causes fat to separate from the chocolate. This may be due to overheating, over-mixing, or the accidental introduction of liquid or steam. The chocolate first appears greasy, then fat migrates to the surface. The problem can be easily remedied, so never discard a broken-looking batch. Pour all of the contents onto a sheet of plastic wrap, seal it, and set it aside.

Once set, the fat will turn white and harden into a waxy surface film. It is easier to spot the waxy white coating against a dark color of modeling chocolate like the blue batch above. On white or light-colored batches, it is harder to notice. To the touch, it feels like a soft crust. Do not knead modeling chocolate at this stage. Kneading will mix the crust into the batch, creating a grainy texture and appearance.

Three Solutions to the Broken Emulsion Problem

1. Early Kneading: When a batch of modeling chocolate loses its emulsion during production, the easiest way to correct the problem is to knead at the stage when it is firm enough to handle but not so firm that the fat on the surface has hardened into a crust. This usually occurs within ½–2 hours after production. Beware that kneading too early or too often may agitate the chocolate further. It must be at least firm enough to hold its shape before handling.

2. Melt Just the Fat: If the crusty fat layer has fully or partially set, microwave the batch in its plastic wrap on both sides for 5 seconds each or just long enough to soften the shell. Alternatively, unwrap it and place it on a sheet pan in a warm oven for 30 seconds or more. Pinch all around the outside of the chocolate to be sure the rind has softened adequately; it should squish between the fingers with no resistance. Knead the batch against a tabletop with the palms of the hands until smooth and no longer oily. Avoid overheating or overworking the chocolate, which may cause it to separate again.

3. Last Resort: If the crusty fat layer accidentally gets kneaded into the chocolate resulting in a batch that is contaminated by little white bits, heat the modeling chocolate in its plastic wrap in the microwave for 5–10 seconds on either side or until soft throughout. Then work it thoroughly on a tabletop with a bench scraper, pulling small amounts under the blade and dragging them against the surface of the table to mince the hard bits into a pulp. Additionally or alternatively, pass the entire batch through a pasta roller or sheeter on the narrowest setting. Doing this several times will pulverize the majority of the bits. The batch may never be completely smooth again but it will be useable enough for most purposes.

Modeling Chocolate that is too Hard

If a batch is freshly set, it may be difficult to work with at first. Break off and knead small chunks by hand until they are malleable.

If the environment is under 60°F (15°C), modeling chocolate may become brittle and difficult to work with. Knead it by hand vigorously until it comes to a more workable temperature and consistency. Alternatively, microwave it in its plastic wrap on high for three-second bursts, turning it over between bursts, or unwrap it and place it on a sheet pan in a warm oven to heat for 30 seconds or until soft. Then knead it until the heat is evenly distributed. Be careful not to overheat chocolate or it may seize or scorch.

Modeling Chocolate that is too Dry/Crumbly

If not enough sugar syrup is present in proportion to the chocolate, the result will be a dry, crumbly consistency. If this is the case, knead in more syrup one teaspoon at a time. If it is too difficult to knead, gently soften the chocolate in the microwave or over a double boiler before adding the additional sugar syrup.

If rolled modeling chocolate is improperly stored, for instance, if it is left out unwrapped for more than a few hours or is stored for days/weeks/months in plastic wrap or a non-airtight vessel, it will dry out. To rehydrate it, knead in more sugar syrup, ½ teaspoon at a time, until the desired consistency returns.

Modeling Chocolate that is too Soft/Sticky

If the modeling chocolate has just been handled, it may be too soft to work with. Between stages of handling, it must be allowed to cool and reset.

If the work environment is too hot and/or humid, technical difficulties may occur. A cool 60–65°F (15–18°C) environment is vital. If possible, install an air conditioner near the work station. Be sure to properly vent the unit's exhaust. Alternatively, keep two to three metal sheet pans in the freezer and rotate them in and out of the cold as needed to create a chilled work surface. Be sure to always insert parchment paper between chocolate and pan to prevent condensation from wetting the chocolate. Alternatively, keep an ice-cold freezer pack close by to cool hands and fingers.

If too much sugar syrup is present in proportion to chocolate, a batch will be overly soft. To correct an overly soft batch, knead in one to two tablespoons of melted chocolate.

If some other form of invert sugar was used in place of corn syrup or glucose (such as honey, molasses, agave, treacle, golden syrup, or simple syrup) the result is often a sticky mass that must be discarded.

If a significant amount of food coloring is added to a batch of modeling chocolate, it may soften the overall texture. See Coloring on page 20 for more on this topic.

Work Station
Tools & Gadgets

The ideal working environment for rolling and modeling chocolate is a cool, 60–65°F (15–18°C), dry room with clean surfaces and equipment. Do not work directly in sunlight. Minimize contact with moisture and humidity. The optimal tabletop is clean, smooth, and made from a stone that retains cool temperatures such as marble, glass, or granite. Stainless steel or laminate countertops are adequate. Avoid wood, as the grain is too porous. Working in close proximity to the cool blast of an air conditioner aids in efficiency and ease of handling.

Rolled Modeling Chocolate Equipment

The following seven items are used to execute nearly all of the techniques found in this book:

Parchment Paper, ideally quilon-coated, full sheet pan liners measuring 16x24 inches (41x 61cm)

Silicone Rolling Pins, optimal for hand-rolling modeling chocolate because of their seamless, poreless surface. It's handy to have a large and small size.

Blush Brush, for dusting chocolate with cornstarch

Cornstarch, to prevent sticking

Craft Utility Knife (a.k.a. Xacto knife)

Roller Cutter, preferably mini 4-inch (10 cm)

Pasta Machine, with countertop clamp and adjustable setting for rolling thin sheets of chocolate.
[**Expert Option:** A commercial sheeter]

Cutters, Veiners & Formers

For cutting and adding texture to rolled modeling chocolate decorations.

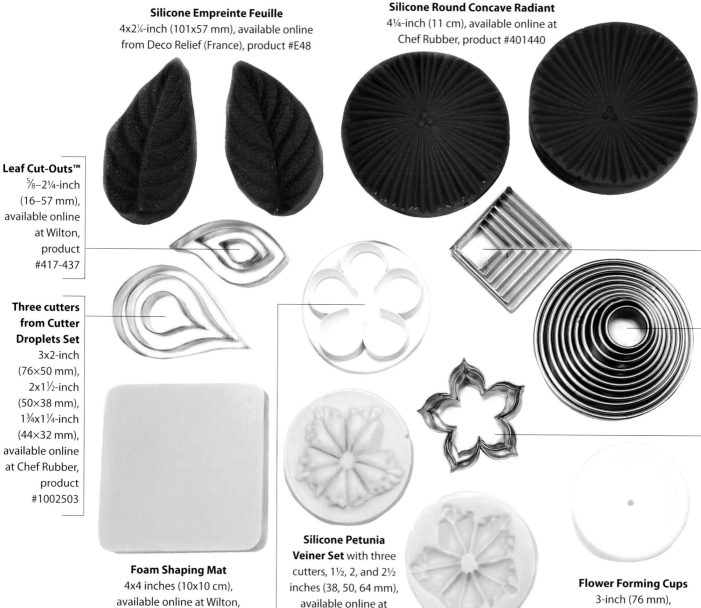

Silicone Empreinte Feuille
4x2¼-inch (101x57 mm), available online from Deco Relief (France), product #E48

Silicone Round Concave Radiant
4¼-inch (11 cm), available online at Chef Rubber, product #401440

Leaf Cut-Outs™
⅝–2¼-inch (16–57 mm), available online at Wilton, product #417-437

Three cutters from Cutter Droplets Set
3x2-inch (76×50 mm), 2x1½-inch (50×38 mm), 1¾x1¼-inch (44×32 mm), available online at Chef Rubber, product #1002503

Square Cutter set of seven, ¾ to 2¼ inches (19–57 mm), available online at Kerekes, product #395674

Ateco Plain Round Cutters eleven piece set, ¾ to 3⅝ inches (19–92 mm), available online at Ateco, product #5357

Silicone Petunia Veiner Set with three cutters, 1½, 2, and 2½ inches (38, 50, 64 mm), available online at Global Sugar Art, product #19028

Foam Shaping Mat
4x4 inches (10x10 cm), available online at Wilton, product #1907-9704

Silicone Petunia Veiner Set with three cutters, 1½, 2, and 2½ inches (38, 50, 64 mm), available online at Global Sugar Art, product #19028

Flower Forming Cups
3-inch (76 mm), available online at Wilton, product #1907-118

Five-Petal Cutter
plastic 2.95-inch (75 mm), available online at Sugarcraft, product #FP899

Plunger Cutters

Plunger cutters are more efficient than traditional cutters at producing shapes and decorations.

Kemper Sugarpaste Pattern Cutters
five-piece square set, ¼ to $^{11}/_{16}$-inch
(6–17 mm), find online at Kerekes,
product code: KSQUARE

PME Blossom Plunger Cutters
¼, ⅜, and 1 inch (6, 10, 25 mm),
find online at Sugarcraft, product
#NNFB550/FB550/43-550FB)

**Kemper Sugarpaste
Pattern Cutters**
three piece circle set,
$^5/_{16}$ to ¾-inch
(8–19 mm), find online
at Kerekes, Product
code: KCIRCLE

Silicone Formers
Large, Medium, and Small

These formers are the best for storing rolled modeling chocolate flowers and decorations because they are nonstick and bendy in a way that makes it easy to release shapes. They can also be used for a myriad of other confectionery molding and baking techniques.

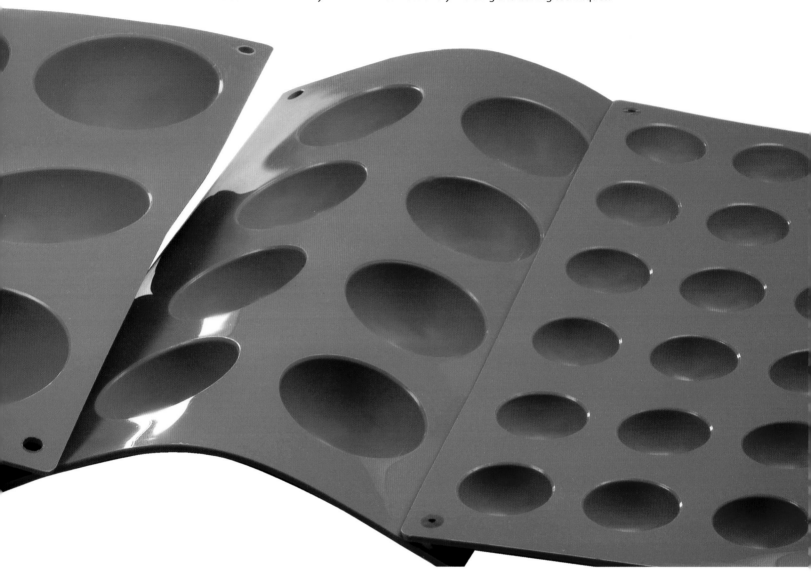

Sculpting and Decorating Tools

These are the tools that are referenced the most in this book.

Rubber Gloves to prevent dying hands when working with colors.

Styrofoam Brick wrapped in plastic wrap, to anchor figurines in process.

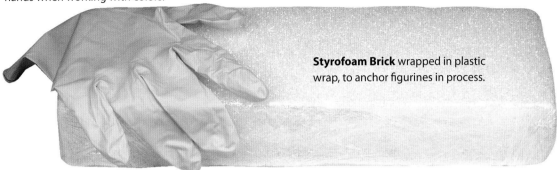

Yard/Meter Stick to measure and trim rolled modeling chocolate.

Flexible Measuring Tape for measuring contoured cakes.

Spoon for thinning edges of rolled modeling chocolate.

Pointed Sculpting Implement

Clay Extruder for forming ropes and strings of modeling chocolate. The basic load-and-push variety is the easiest to clean and use. I recommend Sculpey® brand, which comes with a collection of dies.

Round Piping Tips for cutting small circles of rolled modeling chocolate

Double-Ended Ball Tool

Flat Sculpting Implement

Scissors

Pointed/Blunt Sculpting Implement

Small Paintbrush

Extruder Dies 1 mm and ½ cm for use in the clay extruder.

White Sparkle

Disco Dust

Pearl Dust

Gold Dust

Styrofoam Balls for building figurines.

Fondant Smoother for smoothing rolled modeling chocolate inlays and wraps.

Lollypop Sticks for building figurines.

Round Microcutters for cutting small circles of rolled modeling chocolate.

See the Wicked Goodies website for direct purchasing links to these products.

Rolling & Wrapping

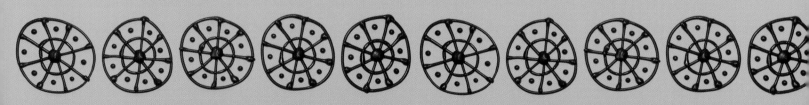

Rolling By Hand

1. Knead the modeling chocolate until it is pliable but still firm. Form it into a flat patty.

2. Using a blush brush, lightly dust the top and bottom surfaces of the chocolate with cornstarch.

3. Roll the chocolate out evenly atop parchment paper with a silicone rolling pin.

4. To achieve thin sheets, roll modeling chocolate between two pieces of parchment paper. If the parchment buckles as the chocolate stretches, peel it back to release the tension before resuming again.

5. Once rolled, the chocolate will be soft, sticky, and sandwiched between two pieces of parchment paper. Allow it to rest for 10–30 minutes or until firm enough to handle. Alternatively, place it in front of the cool blast of an air conditioner for about five minutes.

Expert Option: Use immediately but work swiftly to minimize hand contact.

6. Once the rolled modeling chocolate is firm like a fruit roll-up, peel and pull the top piece of parchment away. *Note* Attempting to pull chocolate off parchment may cause it to tear. Instead, peel parchment away from chocolate.

7. Using a blush brush, dust the top of the rolled modeling chocolate lightly with cornstarch.

8. Return the parchment paper to the top side and flip the sheet so that the bottom side faces up.

9. Peel the remaining layer of stuck paper off the chocolate and brush that side with cornstarch as well. The chocolate should no longer stick to the paper on either side and, at this point, it can be moved, formed, or cut into decorations of any variety.

Rolling with a Machine

Because modeling chocolate has little elasticity, it can be rolled exceptionally thin for fine decorations. In high volume operations, chocolate may be rolled in a commercial sheeter using traditional all-purpose flour as the dusting agent. For home kitchens to moderate-sized bakeries, passing chocolate through a hand-cranked pasta machine using cornstarch as the dusting agent yields formidable results.

Tip 1: Always roll chocolate out onto parchment paper. Laying fresh chocolate sheets directly on the surface of a table may cause sticking.

Tip 2: When rolling, use chocolate that is cool and firm. If chocolate is too warm, it may cling to the gears and bunch underneath the rollers. If too cold, it may shatter or resist rolling altogether. Knead the chocolate to warm it up and rest it to cool it down as needed.

1. Begin by kneading the modeling chocolate until it is pliable but still firm. Flatten it into a ½-inch (13 mm) thick patty with the palm of the hand. Pass it through the machine on a thick setting.

2. Fold the chocolate back into shape and then pass it through on increasingly thinner settings until the desired thinness is achieved. Avoid contact with the edges of the rollers, where chocolate may get stuck.

3. When the desired thinness is achieved, place rolled sheets of chocolate onto parchment paper, spacing them ½-inch (13 mm) apart.

4. Holes or flaws in the texture are common and okay at this stage. Remove any unwanted particulates with the tip of a knife. Plug any holes and reinforce any thin areas with extra scraps of chocolate.

5. Place another piece of parchment on top so that the rolled modeling chocolate is sandwiched between two pieces of paper. Roll firmly over the top with a rolling pin. This step will give the sheets a smooth finish and sheen.

6. Proceed with Steps 5–9 of Rolling by Hand (see page 35).

Machine Maintenance

When rolling many colors in a row through a machine, work from lightest to darkest to prevent dark flecks from infiltrating lighter colors.

Keep rollers clean and free of debris by passing an old piece of white modeling chocolate through between uses. Use the old chocolate like a lint brush, periodically running it between the rollers to pull flecks of color and stuck chocolate from the gears.

To perform a deeper cleaning of the rollers, open them to the widest setting and rub them thoroughly with a damp plastic scouring pad. Pass a paper towel through the machine several times on increasingly thinner settings to absorb the moisture and residues left behind. Allow the machine to dry for several hours hours before using it again.

Preserving Sheets & Decorations

Rolled modeling chocolate can remain exposed to the air for a much longer time than fondant without forming an elephant skin. However, if it is left uncovered, it will eventually grow stiff and brittle. To preserve the softness and pliability of rolled modeling chocolate decorations, cover them with plastic wrap. Store them on metal sheet pans in a cool place out of sunlight. To store rolled modeling chocolate for a number of days, sandwich it directly between two pieces of plastic wrap (parchment paper, over time, will draw moisture from rolled modeling chocolate). For the best pliancy and performance, use chocolate within hours of rolling.

Rolling Out Large Sheets

If a commercial sheeter is available, one can roll chocolate to any size or thickness with ease. If a pasta machine is available, smaller pieces may be patched together to create larger ones. If only a rolling pin is available, large sheets may be rolled by hand between two pieces of parchment paper. However, it is easiest to achieve a consistent thickness using a machine.

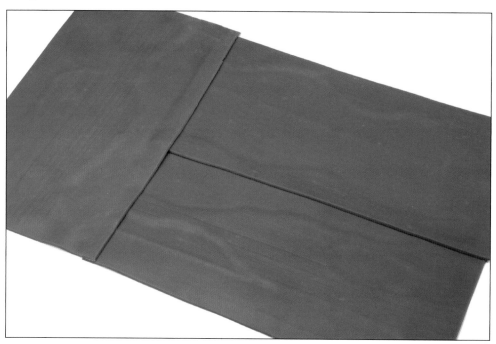

Patching Together Pieces to Form Sheets

1. Begin by rolling out long strips of chocolate.

2. With a roller cutter, trim any rough edges. Ball up the scraps for reuse.

3. Piece together the strips, overlapping their edges by ¼ inch (6 mm) until the desired size and shape is achieved.

4. Roll the chocolate between two pieces of parchment paper with a plastic rolling pin to smooth out the uneven surfaces and bind seams.

5. Proceed with Steps 5–9 of Rolling by Hand. (see page 35)

Cake Wrapping Using the Paneling Method

This technique may be used as an alternative to covering a cake in fondant. The chocolate provides a smooth protective surface to the cake. It also allows for more adventurous patterning. This particular cake is 8 inches (20 cm) in diameter and 6 inches (15 cm) tall, but this technique can be used to cover any size cake: cylinder, square, hexagon, etc.

Note: Because the cake is flipped onto every one of its sides to execute this method, it must first be well chilled. Use real buttercream (recipe, pg. 150) to coat the cake. When chilled, the butter in the frosting forms a hard shell that makes turning a cake upside down and on its side quite possible.

1. Using a flexible measuring tape,

measure the surfaces of the cake in order to approximate the dimensions of the chocolate sheets needed. For a cylinder cake of this size, one 9-inch (23 cm) diameter circle is needed to cover the top and one 25x7-inch (64x18 cm) long sheet is needed to wrap around the sides with an extra inch (25 mm) all around for insurance.

Items Needed

- Finished cake with a finish coat of vanilla buttercream (see recipe, page 150), refrigerator cold
- Flexible measuring tape
- White modeling chocolate plus yellow, orange, and bittersweet for the leopard print pattern.
- Rolled modeling chocolate equipment (page 29)
- Ruler or straight edge
- Platter or scrap of cardboard at least 9 inches (23 cm) in diameter

2. Roll out a 9-inch (23 cm) diameter circle of white modeling chocolate to ¹⁄₁₆-inch (1.6 mm) thickness. Cover it in plastic wrap and set it aside for Step 8.

3. Roll out a ⅛-inch thick, 25 inches long, 7 inches wide (3 mm x 64 cm x18 cm) rectangle to wrap around the sides. If executing the leopard print pattern, see Leopard Print (page 94).

4. Flip the rectangle so that its finished side is face down on a piece of parchment paper. Using a ruler/straight edge as a guide, trim one long side with a roller cutter so that the edge is clean and straight.

5. Beginning on one end of the strip, roll the sides of the chilled cake like a wheel over the chocolate. Roll it so that the top edge of the cake runs flush with the trimmed edge of chocolate. Use the parchment paper to pull and roll the chocolate onto the cake. **Expert Option:** Roll the strip of modeling chocolate around a rolling pin then unroll it vertically onto the edges of a standing cake.

6. Turn the cake so that the flush edge is facing away and the rough edge is facing toward you. Slowly roll the cake again, this time trimming the excess chocolate from the remaining side. Allow the rough ends to overlap where the wrap meets itself.

7. Turn the cake right-side up with the rough edge toward you. With a craft utility knife, cut through the overlapping ends to create a straight seam. Pull away the excess.

8. Place the better side of the 9-inch (23 cm) white circle of rolled modeling chocolate from Step 2 face down on parchment paper. Invert the top side of the cake into the white chocolate and trim around the edges with a craft utility knife. Angle the knife away from the cake while trimming to avoid gouging the finished sides.

9. Slide the cake off the edge of the table onto a second piece of cardboard lined with parchment paper. Flip the cake right-side up onto a platter or piece of cardboard. Cover the cake's surface tightly in plastic wrap and return it immediately to the refrigerator.
Note To wrap modeling chocolate around the sides of a square cake, bend one continuous sheet around the sides, or alternatively, cut a separate panel for each side and apply them individually.

Cake Wrapping Using the Draping Method

The draping method is handy for contoured shapes. Here, the rolled modeling chocolate wrap gives a jalapeño cake the red and wrinkled look of a hot pepper's skin. This cake was served on a hot day to a pool party near the California-Mexico border.

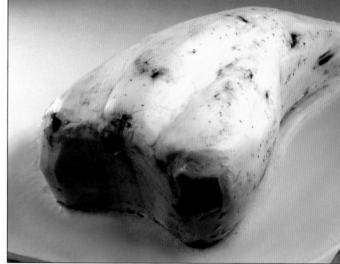

Items Needed

- Crumb-coated cake, refrigerator cold
- Red modeling chocolate
- Rolled modeling chocolate equipment (page 29)
- Plastic bowl scraper

1. Roll the red modeling chocolate out to ⅛-inch (3 mm) thickness. Allow it to rest in a cool place for 30 minutes or until it is firm and easy to handle.

2. Peel back the parchment and dust both sides of the sheet generously with cornstarch (as long as the cornstarch is not caked, it will vanish).

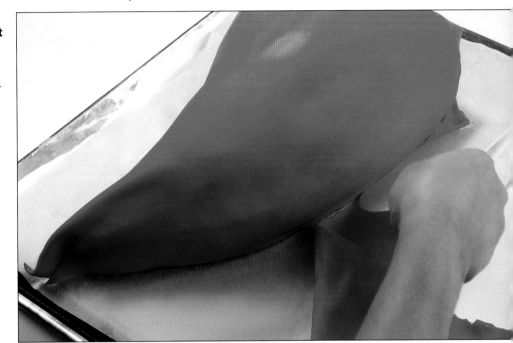

3. Slide the sheet off the parchment and onto the cake.

4. Fit the sheet loosely around the cake.

5. Press the rounded edge of a plastic bowl scraper around the bottom edge of the cake to trim the excess and tuck any rough edges out of sight.

6. Cover the cake's surface tightly in plastic wrap and return it immediately to the refrigerator.

To form a stem, cut a thick star shape and roll out the ends until thin. Hollow out the center and add a twisted vine piece.

Present Cake Wrapping

The classic present cake is appropriate for almost any occasion. Modeling chocolate is especially well suited for patterned wrapping and fine bows. This particular cake is a 7x7x7-inch (18x18x18cm) cube.

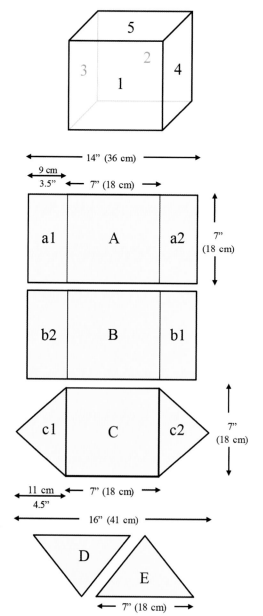

Items Needed

- Finished square/rectangular cake with a finish coat of vanilla buttercream, refrigerator cold
- White, yellow, orange, and red modeling chocolate
- Rolled modeling chocolate equipment (page 29)
- Assorted square plunger cutters
- Ruler or straight edge

Note: The five exposed sides of the cake cube are referred to herein by number, with 5 being the top side of the cake, 1 and 4 being the front-facing sides, and 2 and 3 being the back-facing sides. A–E are the chocolate wrapping paper components.

1. Roll out sheets of white modeling chocolate to ⅛-inch (3 mm) thickness. Form two identical 15x8-inch (38x20 cm) rectangles, one 17x8-inch (43x20 cm) pointed rectangle, and two triangles, allowing the extra inch (25 mm) all around for insurance. For a confetti effect, follow the instructions for inlaid patterns using square plunger cutters (page 91).

2. Cut D and E from one rectangle or square. Set them aside.

3. Using a ruler as a guide, trim one long side of A with a craft utility knife so that the edge is clean and straight. Flip A so that its finished side is facing down on a piece of parchment paper.

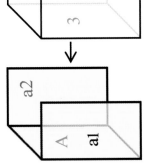

4. As per the paneling method (pg. 39), **place the cake with side 3 facing down** in the center of A, aligning the trimmed side of A with the top edge of the cake.

5. Wrap the wings a1 and a2 halfway around sides 1 and 2 respectively.

6. Trim the excess.

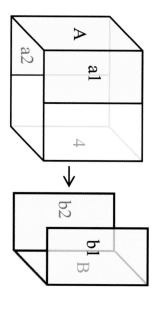

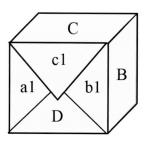

7. Repeat Steps 3–5 on panel B, wrapping it around side 4 of the cube. Wrap the wings b1 and b2 around the remaining exposed halves of sides 1 and 2 respectively. Trim the excess so that a1 meets b1 and a2 meets b2 (the seams will eventually be concealed by the ribbon). Immediately turn the cake right-side up.

8. Position D and E at the base of sides 1 and 2 respectively.

9. Repeat Steps 3–5 on panel C, wrapping it over side 5 so that the triangular wings, c1 and c2, extend onto sides 1 and 2 respectively.

10. Cover the cake's surface tightly in plastic wrap and return it immediately to the refrigerator.

Bows & Ribbons

The trick to a full-looking bow is to cut wider strips for the ears than for the rest of the bow/ribbon components.

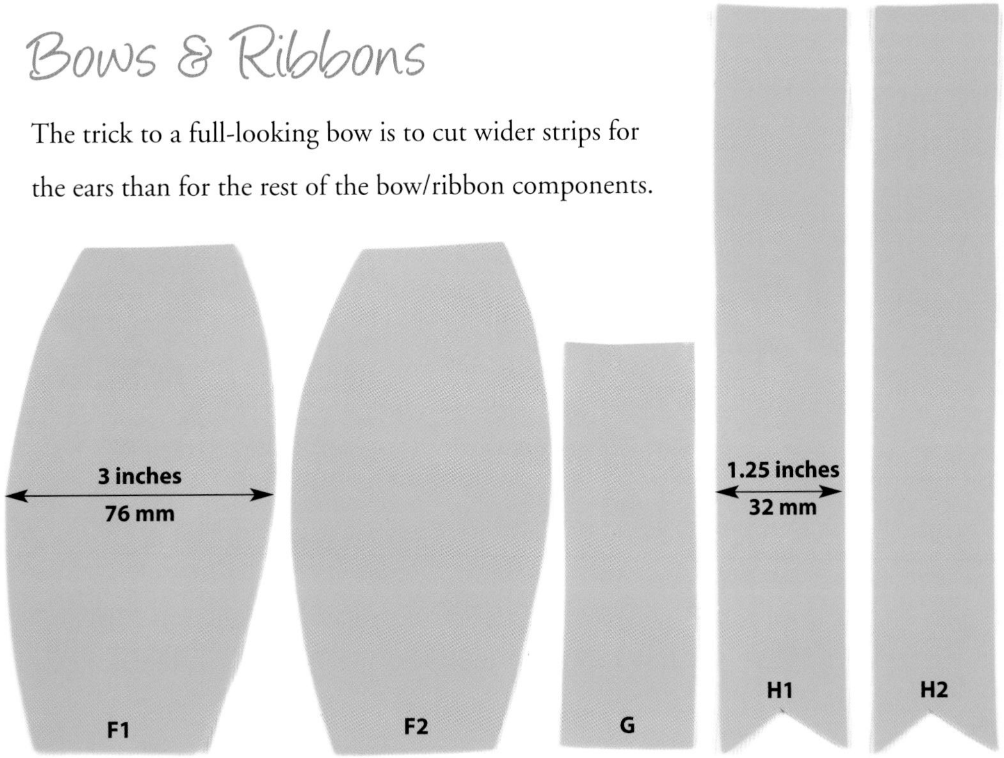

3 inches
76 mm

1.25 inches
32 mm

F1 F2 G H1 H2

1. Roll out the blue modeling chocolate to $\frac{1}{16}$-inch (1.6 mm) thickness. Roll to a width of at least 22 inches (56 cm).

2. Cut two 22-inch long, $1\frac{1}{4}$-inch wide strips (56 cm x32 mm) for ribbons. Set them aside.

3. Cut the bow components F–H as shown. G–H must be the same width as the ribbon: $1\frac{1}{4}$ inches (32 mm) wide. F1–F2, the loops of the bow, should be twice as wide as the ribbon: 3 inches (76 mm) at the widest part with a slight taper at the ends.

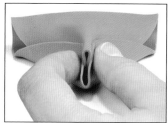

4. Fold over and pinch the tapered ends of F1 and F2 so that they join in the middle. Pull the loops open and prop them up.

Work swiftly to minimize handling at this stage. Set the loops aside to firm up for at least one hour before handling again.

5. Wrap the two ribbon components from Step 2 over the cake in a cross. Trim the excess with a craft utility knife.

6. Place the bow's ends, H1 and H2, on the cake as shown, with the straight ends meeting on top of the cake at the junction where the ribbons cross. Drape them loosely over the edges of the cake and curl them up at the tips.

7. Fold the center band G, into a loop wide enough to form the bow's center. Place it seam-side down where the ribbons cross.

8. Tuck the pinched ends of F1 and F2 into either opening of G. Secure any loose parts with a dab of buttercream to hold the bow in place.

9. To form a tag, roll chocolate to ⅛-inch (3 mm) thickness and cut it into the above shape. Punch a hole into the narrow end using a round piping tip or small ½-cm diameter round cutter. Pipe an inscription with melted white chocolate.

Ruffles & Pleats

This wedding cake was designed to look like the bride's gown, which had a ruffled skirt and pleated bodice. The top tier includes a pearl choker and bouquet of fabric flowers to represent aspects of the bride's outfit. It was comprised of three cylindrical tiers measuring 6, 9, and 12 inches (15, 23, and 30 cm) in diameter and 4 inches (10 cm) in height, all decorated in ivory.

Ruffles

For the 12-inch (30 cm) diameter, 4-inch (10 cm) tall cylinder tier.

Items Needed

- 12 inch cylinder cake with a finish coat of vanilla butter-cream, refrigerator cold
- Large cake drum or equivalent serving platform, in this case, 15 inches (38 cm)
- White modeling chocolate, at least 2 batches
- Rolled modeling chocolate equipment (page 29)
- Stainless steel spoon

1. Roll out white modeling chocolate sheets to ¹⁄₁₆-inch (1.6 mm) thickness.

2. Cut the sheets the long way to make 2½-inch (64 mm) wide strips. To cover this particular cake, the total length of strips needed is approximately 40 feet (12.2 meters).

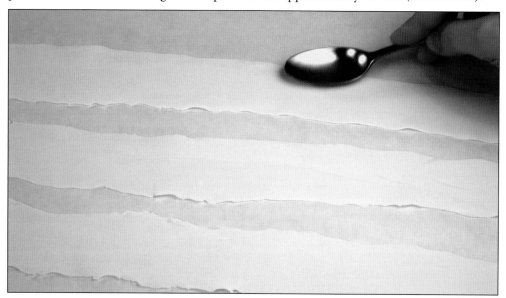

3. Rub the rounded backside of a spoon over one long edge of each strip. Run the spoon from the inside of the rolled modeling chocolate out until the edges are thin to the point of shredding. Cover the finished strips with plastic wrap until ready to use.

4. Remove the 12-inch (30 cm) cake tier from the refrigerator. Begin by winching a strip to form a ruffle that runs around the entire base of the drum. Lay it so that the thin edge points out. Wherever one strip ends and another begins, carry on with the same curved pattern of the ruffle. When the chocolate comes full circle, trim it so that the ends meet.

5. Add a second ruffle atop the first, this time pressing its top edge into the sides of the frosted cake. Add dabs of buttercream if necessary to help it stick. Winch and press the chocolate with the pad of the thumb into the buttercream. Take care to maintain consistent height around the cake's circumference.

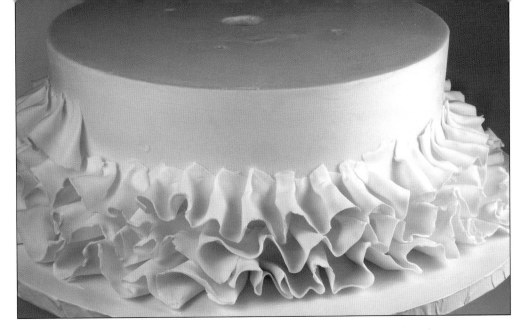

6. Add two more layers so that only the top inch of the cake's sides remain bare.

7. Just below the top edge of the cake, add a ruffle that is winched at the bottom and points upward in the opposite direction of the other ruffles.

8. Add one final ruffle into the remaining gap, pressing into its center so that it flares out at both the top and bottom. *Note* This particular ruffle must be thinned on both edges since both will show.

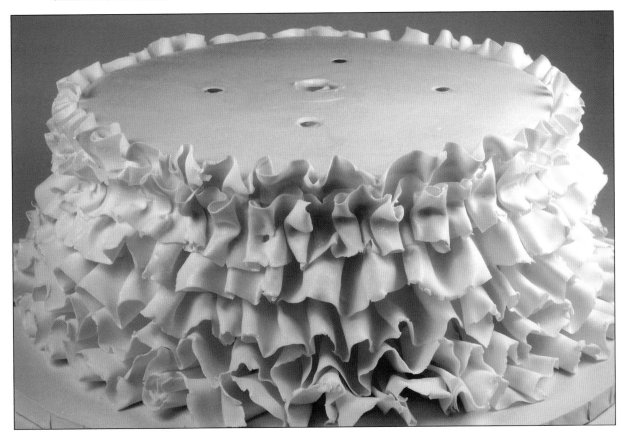

Pleats

For the 9-inch (23 cm) diameter, 4-inch (10 cm) tall cylinder cake.

Items Needed

- 9-inch cylinder cake with a finish coat of vanilla buttercream, refrigerator cold
- Four 6-inch (15 cm) diameter corrugated circles or alternatively, a 6-inch (15 cm) diameter cake pan
- Toothpick or pointed sculpting implement
- Flexible measuring tape
- White modeling chocolate, 1 full batch
- Rolled modeling chocolate equipment (page 29)
- Ruler or straight edge
- Pearl dust

1. With the toothpick, etch a 6-inch (15 cm) circle in the center of the 9-inch (23 cm) top surface of the cake using one of the 6-inch (15 cm) diameter corrugated circles as a guide.

2. With flexible measuring tape, measure the length on a diagonal from the edge of the etched circle to the base of the tier. For this 9-inch (23 cm) cake, the distance is approximately 8 inches (20 cm).

3. Roll out 9-inch (23 cm) wide sheets of white chocolate, allowing the extra inch (25 mm) for insurance.

4. Dust the sheets liberally on both sides with cornstarch.

5. Using a ruler as a guide, cut horizontal strips that are each ½-inch (13 mm) wide.

6. Dust the top sides of the strips with pearl dust using a blush brush. Cover them with plastic wrap and set them aside until ready to use.

7. Remove the 9-inch (23 cm) tier from the refrigerator and elevate it 1 inch (25 mm) off the table or turntable using the 6-inch (15 cm) diameter corrugated circles.

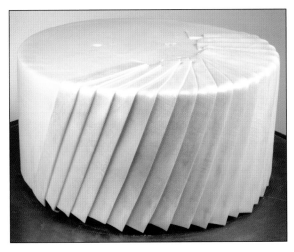

8. Begin placing the rolled modeling chocolate strips on the cake one at a time so that they overlap just slightly and cover the entire surface area of the cake. Due to the angle, a jagged hem will form at the base of the cake.

9. As the pleating approaches full circle, make any necessary adjustments to the angle gradually so that when the first and last strip meet, they are on the same bias.

10. With a craft utility knife, trim the jagged hem all the way around the cake flush with the bottom. Remove the 6-inch (15 cm) diameter corrugated circles from underneath the cake.

11. Place one of the 6-inch (15 cm) diameter corrugated circles on the top center of the cake and trim around it using a craft utility knife, cutting though all the excess strip ends that are bunched towards the middle. Remove the cardboard and remove the scraps of chocolate from the center of the cake.

12. Seal the cake in plastic wrap and return it to the refrigerator.

To read how to make the fabric roses on top of the cake, see page 72.

To read how to pipe the pearl choker cascade design, see pg. 144.

To learn how to use wood dowels in stacked cakes, read the tutorial on the Wicked Goodies website, www.WickedGoodies.com

Swag / Drapery

This cake was designed for the thirtieth birthday party of a woman who grew up in the 80s. For her cake, she requested zebra-stripe swag and funky neon bangles in chocolate. The design included 4-inch (10 cm) tall tapered tiers whose bases measure 5, 8, and 11 inches (13, 20, and 28 cm) in diameter. Rolled modeling chocolate is the ideal medium for swag and drapery effects since it can be rolled as sheer as gauze.

Swag/drapery technique works best with chocolate that is on the soft/supple side. It is especially important when executing swag to keep rolled modeling chocolate dusted on both sides with cornstarch to prevent it from sticking to itself.

Items Needed

- Flexible measuring tape
- White and black modeling chocolate
- Rolled modeling chocolate equipment (page 29)
- 2 long wooden dowels, at least 32 inches long (81 cm) and 1 cm thick

1. Use the flexible measuring tape to measure the circumference of the bottom of each tier to determine how many lengths of chocolate are needed to fully wrap the cake. Add at least a few extra inches for insurance. In this case the length needed is 80 inches (2 meters).

2. Roll out white modeling chocolate to ¹⁄₁₆-inch (1.6 mm) thickness. Create long strips that are 6 inches (15 cm) wide. For the zebra-stripe pattern, follow the instructions on page 99. Allow the rolled modeling chocolate to rest until it is just firm enough to handle.

3. Brush both sides of the rolled modeling chocolate thoroughly with cornstarch.

4. Arrange two dowels on top of a full sheet of parchment paper, spacing them ½-inch (13 mm) apart.

5. Drape the chocolate over the dowels the long way.

6. Run a fingertip through the grooves, gently combing the chocolate into a wavy shape.

7. Pull the dowels out from underneath the chocolate. The chocolate should hold its shape. **Expert Option:** Fold the rolled modeling chocolate sheet by hand, omitting use of the dowels.

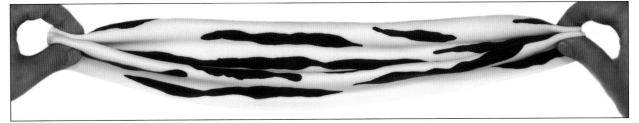

8. Bunch each end of the swag and pinch between fingertips. Lift and swiftly transfer it onto the cake, folding any tattered edges underneath. Tuck ends around one another so that they remain out of sight.

Eighties Accessories

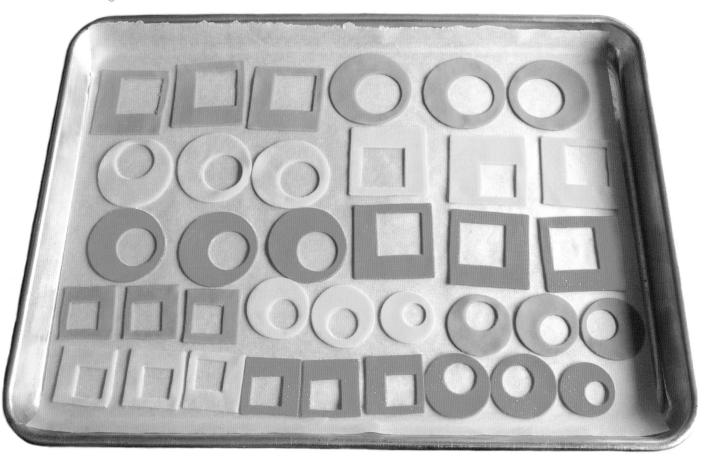

Items Needed

- Pink, yellow, and blue modeling chocolate
- Rolled modeling chocolate equipment (page 29)
- Nested round and square cutter sets
- Disco dust

1. Roll out the modeling chocolate colors to $\frac{1}{16}$-inch (1.6 mm) thickness.

2. Using the bigger cutters from the nested cutter sets, first cut medium- and large-size circles and squares.

3. Using the smaller cutters, cut pieces from the centers. Cut them off-center.

4. Dust the shapes with disco dust.

5. Press them onto the sides of the cake gently, distributing them evenly all over.

Flowers & Foliage

Basic 3D Buds

This common and easy cake decoration that is so popular with fondant can also be executed with rolled modeling chocolate. Where fondant blossoms tend to look chunky, rolled modeling chocolate blossoms can be shaped to the thinness of real petals.

Items Needed

- Modeling chocolate, any color
- Rolled modeling chocolate equipment (page 29)
- Small blossom plunger cutter
- Foam shaping mat
- Small ball tool
- Small silicone molds
- Parchment paper cone (or piping bag with small round tip) filled with vanilla buttercream

1. Roll out chocolate to ¹⁄₁₆-inch (1.6 mm) thickness.

2. Cut small buds from each color using plunger cutters. Plunger cutters are the most efficient hand method for producing a large volume of small decorations like flower buds. This style of cutter is particularly useful for stamping out rolled modeling chocolate shapes as it enables one to lift, move, and release the chocolate without ever touching it with the hands.

Ordinary cookie or fondant cutters also work for punching out shapes with modeling chocolate.

To release the chocolate from small molds, gently press the center of the bud with a blunt tool, like the back end of a paintbrush.

3. **Working atop a foam shaping mat** dusted with cornstarch, rub the double-ended ball tool in a circular motion over each petal to thin the edges. This will cause them to curl slightly.

Expert Option: Omit the foam shaping mat and execute Steps 3–4 in the palm of the hand.

4. **Press the ball tool** into the center of the bud and rub again in a circular motion, stretching the flower into a concave, budding shape.

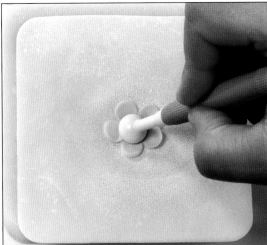

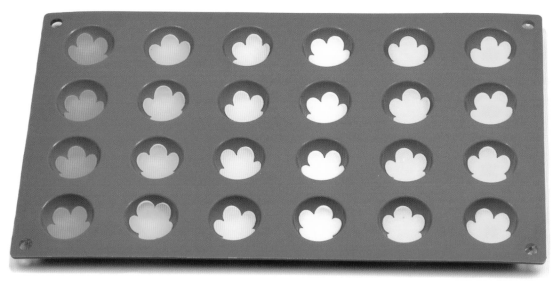

5. Store the flower buds in silicone formers so that they hold a tight, curved shape. Allow them to dry uncovered for at least one hour before handling again. Flowers can be made a week or more in advance of use.

6. When it comes time to decorate the cake with buds, pipe a dot of buttercream onto the back of each flower for glue, then press it gently onto the cake. Work swiftly and decisively, as chocolate flower buds will melt if over-handled.

7. Once all the flowers are secured on the cake, pipe small buttercream pearls in the center of each one.

Fairy Flowers

This wedding cake, fit for a midsummer night's dream, was served at an wedding that took place in a traditional Irish pub in San Diego, California. The bride and groom asked that I design the cake around the whimsical ceramic topper of a fairy princess being kissed by a prince (see end of instructions for topper purchasing information). The cake is finished in chocolate buttercream and draped with petal-thin fairy flowers crafted in rolled modeling chocolate.

Items Needed

- White and dark blue modeling chocolate
- Rolled modeling chocolate equipment (page 29)
- Small blossom plunger cutter
- Double-ended ball tool
- Foam shaping mat
- 3-inch (76 mm) diameter daisy cutter
- Plastic flower cell formers (large)
- Small paintbrush
- Pearl dust and black petal dust
- 1 rubber glove
- Parchment paper cone (or piping bag with small round tip) filled with vanilla buttercream

1. Combine the white and blue modeling chocolate to create four different hues ranging from a light aqua to a rich royal blue.

2. Roll the chocolate out to ¹⁄₁₆-inch (1.6 mm) thickness.

3. Cut small buds from each color using the basic 3D buds method (pages 58-60).

4. Dust the outside edges of the petals with charcoal black petal dust to cast a midnight shadow. Wear a rubber glove to protect fingers from dye.

5. Brush the petals with pearl dust for sheen.

6. Store the flower buds on small silicone cell formers until ready to use.

7. Repeat the process with big flowers, using larger petal cutters and large plastic cell formers. Drape the edges of the petals over the sides of the cups to curl their tips outward.

Note Normally I recommend silicone cell formers but for this particular method, plastic cell formers are best because they have edges around which the petals can be curled.

8. To create uniform-sized centers for the large flowers, roll out a rope of white modeling chocolate and slice it into thick, uniform-sized coins.

9. Roll each coin into a ball.

10. Flatten each ball into a squat, convex shape using the curved palm of a hand.

11. Using a blush brush, dust the tops of the centers generously with pearl dust for sheen. Rub the tops with a fingertip to achieve a smooth and shiny finish.

12. Affix the centers to the petals using a drop of water as glue if needed.

13. Store the flowers in plastic cell formers in a cool place out of sunlight until they are ready to use. Flowers can be made a week or more in advance of use.

14. When it comes time to decorate the cake, place the large flowers first, draping them over edges and at corners. Position them strategically to conceal any flaws in the cake's finish.

15. Add the small flowers next. Pipe a dot of buttercream onto the back of each one for glue, then gently press them onto the cake. Once all the small flowers are on the cake, pipe small pearls of buttercream into the center of each one.

Note The topper is a Jacqueline Collen-Tarrolly collectible called "Frog Once Loved a Turtle." It sells for about $40 and is available at Magical Omaha as well as on eBay and other online cake topper stores.

Carnations

This cake was designed for a Mexican-themed wedding that took place at the Casa Guadalajara restaurant near the border of California and Mexico. The bride asked that I include an edible version of *los claveles,* or the colorful paper carnations that are featured in fiestas.

These fun and easy flowers can be achieved using a simple rolled modeling chocolate technique.

Items Needed

- Bright palette of colored modeling chocolate
- Rolled modeling chocolate equipment (page 29)
- Small spoon
- Pointed sculpting implement
- Scissors

1. Roll each color of modeling chocolate to $\frac{1}{16}$-inch (1.6 mm) thickness.

2. Trim each color into two strips measuring approximately 16 inches (41 cm) long and 1½ inches (38 mm) wide. Cover the strips in plastic wrap when not in use.

3. Atop parchment paper, rub the back of a spoon in an outward direction to thin one long edge of each strip.

4. Bunch and ruffle strip #1, working from the center of the flower out with the thinned edge facing up. Bunch it haphazardly but with an even amount of space between ruffles. Hold the flower only from the bottom. Work swiftly so as not to overheat the chocolate.

5. Continue ruffling in the same manner with strip #2 until the flower is full and complete.

6. While the chocolate is still soft, use a pointed sculpting implement to rearrange petals if necessary. Leave the finished flower sitting upright on parchment paper—exposed to the air—for a few hours to set.

7. Once the flowers are firm, trim their bottoms using scissors. Store them upright on parchment-lined sheets. Flowers can be made a week or more in advance of use.

See page 144 for instructions on the buttercream dot cascade technique that is also used to decorate this cake.

Petunias

This Mother's Day Cake is in honor of my mom, the constant gardener

1. Roll the red, pink, and white modeling chocolate to ¹⁄₁₆-inch (1.6 mm) thickness.

2. Cut star-shaped parts using the three nesting petunia cutters.

Items Needed

- Red, pink, and white modeling chocolate
- Rolled modeling chocolate equipment (page 29)
- Double-sided silicone petunia veiner set with 3 nesting cutters
- Medium silicone cell formers (optional)

3. Stack the stars so that the largest diameter petals are on the bottom and the smallest are on the top.

4. Lay a piece of parchment paper over the stack and with the heel of a hand, gently flatten the disks together to eliminate seams.

5. Dust the top and bottom of each flattened stack with cornstarch, then press them between a double-sided petunia veiner. Squeeze the sides of the veiner gently to release the chocolate from the grooves.

6. Store flowers in medium silicone cell formers until ready to use. Alternatively, arrange them on parchment-lined sheet pans. Flowers can be made a week or more in advance of use.

Blanket Flowers

The blanket flower is a perennial daisy capable of vibrant and myriad color combinations. Here they were used on a three-and-half-foot tall garden rooster cake that I constructed on TLC's Fabulous Cakes show (S2 E7). On that episode, I demonstrated many of the techniques with rolled modeling chocolate that appear in this book.

Items Needed

- Yellow, orange, pink, red, and maroon modeling chocolate
- Rolled modeling chocolate equipment (page 29)
- Round nested cutter set
- Double-sided silicone lily pad veiner
- Large silicone cell formers

1. Roll each color of modeling chocolate into $\frac{1}{16}$-inch (1.6 mm) thick sheets.

2. Using every other circular cutter in the round nested cutter set, cut four consecutively smaller circles from yellow to orange to pink to red.

3. Stack the petals from largest to smallest.

4. Lay a piece of parchment paper over the stack and with the heel of a hand, gently flatten the disks together to eliminate the seams.

5. Dust each flattened stack with cornstarch and press them between the elements of a double-sided silicone lily pad veiner that are also dusted with cornstarch to prevent sticking. Squeeze the sides of the veiner gently to release the chocolate from the grooves.

6. Store the flowers in large silicone cell formers, allowing them to harden for at least one hour before use. Flowers can be made up to a week in advance of use.

7. To form the flower centers, roll maroon modeling chocolate into ½-inch (13 mm) diameter balls. Press one into the center of each flower to complete the decoration.

8. When it comes time to place the flowers onto the cake, secure them from behind with a large dab of buttercream.

Fabric Roses

This whimsical rose style that is quite popular with fondant can also be executed using rolled modeling chocolate. The same fold-and-roll technique applies. In this case it's used as the flower topper on a wedding cake that resembles the bride's dress.

Items Needed

- White modeling chocolate
- Rolled modeling chocolate equipment (page 29)
- Scissors
- Pearl dust

1. Roll out white modeling chocolate to $\frac{1}{16}$-inch (1.6 mm) thickness.

2. Cut a 5–10-inch long (13–26 cm) tapered strip, depending on the size of the flower desired.

3. Gently fold the strip in half the long way, taking care not to crease the folded edge.

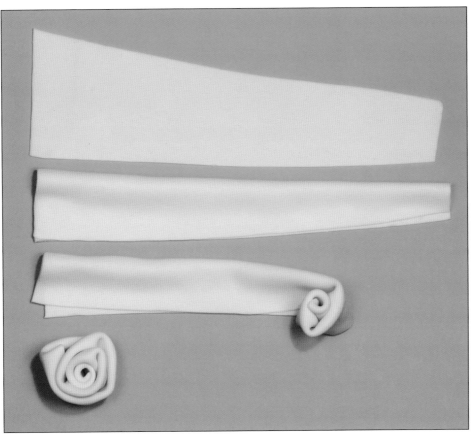

4. Roll the strip into a spiral beginning with the narrower end. Hold the flower only by the bottom. Winch periodically while rolling to create contour and asymmetry.

5. Pinch the bottom and trim any excess with scissors.

6. Brush the flower with pearl dust for sheen.

7. Store flowers upright on parchment paper until ready to use.

8. When it comes time to place the flowers on the cake, secure them with a dab of buttercream.

Authentic Roses

Modeling chocolate is ideal for roses because it can be rolled as thin as lifelike petals. Experienced hands and a cool environment are critical to the success of this technique. Work directly in front of the cool breeze of an air conditioner if possible.

Items Needed

- Orange modeling chocolate
- Rolled modeling chocolate equipment (page 29)
- Round cutter, 2-inch (50 mm) diameter
- Pointed sculpting implement
- Scissors
- Gold luster dust for sheen

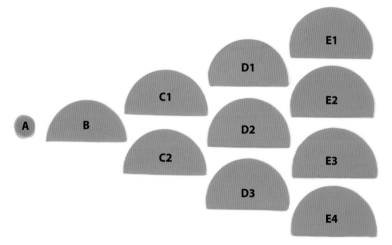

Note Herein, I refer alphanumerically to the components for one large rose in the order that it is assembled beginning with A, the starter piece, and ending with E1 through E4, the outermost petals. For large roses, all 10 petals B through E4 are involved. Small roses are only comprised of B-C-D petals. Rosebuds use only the B-C petals.

1. Roll the orange modeling chocolate out to ¹⁄₁₆-inch (1.6 mm) thickness. Allow 10–30 minutes for it to firm up.

2. Brush both sides of the chocolate sheet with cornstarch.

petal edge

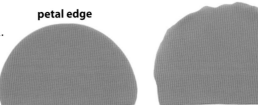

3. Using the round cutter, cut 10 half-moons from the edges of the sheet to form petals B-E.

4. Working atop parchment paper, rub the back end of a spoon over each petal edge. Push the spoon in an outward direction over the edge until fine. Only thin the petal edge; disregard the bottom edge as it will not show once the rose is complete. **Expert Option:** pinch the edge of the petal between two fingertips to thin it.

5. Gather the scraps remaining after cutting out the petals and knead them into a ball. Break off a piece the size of a peanut and form it into a droplet shape, A. Press A onto a piece of parchment paper to flatten its bottom so that it sits upright. A is the hidden center of the rose around which all the other components will be formed. From here on out, hold the flower only at its base and only when necessary. If the rose is over-handled, it may wilt.

6. Wrap B, petal edge up and around A to form an inverted cone with an open point. B is the rose's tight center petal.

7. Wrap C1 halfway around the base of B. Leave the loose flap open. Wrap it so that B's tip lies nestled within. Do not allow B to poke up above the level of C.

8. Tuck the edge of C2 into the junction where B and C1 meet.

9. Wrap C2 around the back of C1, then close C1 around the back of C2 so that ultimately C1 and C2 are cupping one another.

10. With the gentle nudge of a fingertip, push the petal edges of C1 and C2 down and outward to curl them. This completes a rosebud.

rosebud

75

11. Proceed by adding D1-D2-D3 in the same manner as C1-C2. The D petals should come full circle around the base of the flower, with D3 wrapped around the back of D1. This completes a small rose.

12. Continue by adding E1 through E4, encircling them in the same overlapping manner until E4 meets E1. This completes a large rose.

rosebud

small rose

large rose

13. Use a pointed sculpting implement to rearrange any petals if needed. Leave the finished flower sitting upright on parchment paper—exposed to the air—for a few hours to set.

14. Once the petals are stiff, cut the excess from the bottom with a pair of scissors. Trim the bottom straight across for a rose to sit upright or at an angle for a rose to rest on its side.

15. For an iridescent sheen, dust the flowers with gold luster dust using a blush brush.

16. Store finished roses on sheet pans lined with parchment paper. Handle dried roses with care, as they are fragile. Flowers can be made up to a week in advance of use.

- To affix a single rose on a cake, pipe a small dab of buttercream onto the desired spot, then immediately press the backside of the flower into it.

- To affix a spray of roses to the top of a cake, pipe a generous mound of buttercream in the target area, then build—from the bottom up—a dome of large roses with faces radiating outward. Fill in the gaps with small roses, rosebuds, and 3D leaves.

- For a cascading effect down the length of a cake, first arrange the larger roses on ledges and around the base of the cake where maximum support is available. Secure them in place with a dab of buttercream. Pile small roses around and about the large ones. Fill out the vertical elements of the cascade with greenery and rosebuds, using buttercream as glue.

3D Leaves

This was the top tier of a wedding cake that was served at an autumn wedding in New England around that time of year when the acorns fall to the ground and the leaves turn into vibrant reds, oranges, yellows, and greens. Rolled modeling chocolate can be formed into crinkly leaves with the help of a double-sided silicone leaf veiner. One large veiner can be used to press many leaf shapes and sizes as shown below. A good quality veiner combined with some basic leaf cutters is a worthy investment for a cake decorator's tool kit.

Items Needed

- Green modeling chocolate
- Rolled modeling chocolate equipment (page 29)
- Leaf cutter of choice
- Small spoon
- Large double-sided silicone leaf veiner
- Large silicone cell formers (optional)
- Cocoa powder

1. **Roll green modeling chocolate** to $\frac{1}{16}$-inch (1.6 mm) thickness.

2. **Cut a leaf shape** using a leaf cutter.

3. Working atop parchment paper, run the back of a spoon over the edges of the leaf to thin them.

4. Dust the leaf with cornstarch, then press it between the double-sided silicone veiner, also dusted with cornstarch.

5. Remove the leaf from the veiner. Pinch it's center vein to accentuate the crease. Curl the edges to add contour.

6. Arrange the leaves in various positions over a large silicone cell former. Alternatively, position them on a parchment-lined sheet pan. Allow them to dry in a cool place out of sunlight for at least two hours or ideally, overnight.

To add streaks of light and shadow, marblize the modeling chocolate using the linear marble effect (page 83). Then cut the leaf shapes so that the striations run in the direction of the vein.

For a thorny effect, scallop the edges of the leaves using the tip of a small leaf cutter.

To accentuate the veins, brush the leaves with cocoa powder using a blush brush.

Acorns

Items Needed

- Bittersweet and white modeling chocolate
- Rolled modeling chocolate equipment (page 29)
- Double-ended ball tool
- Foam shaping mat
- Small silicone cell former
- Toothpick or pointed sculpting implement
- Small paintbrush
- Cocoa powder
- Gold luster dust

1. Combine one part bittersweet and three parts white modeling chocolate to achieve a mahogany hue for the nut part of the acorn.

2. Roll it into a rope and cut off equal-size portions the size of acorn nuts.

3. Roll the nuts into balls, then roll the balls into egg shapes.

4. Push them down onto parchment paper to flatten them.

5. Roll each nut's tip between two fingertips to narrow the point. Set the nuts aside for about an hour or until firm.

6. To form the caps, roll a small chunk of bittersweet modeling chocolate into a log. Cut equal-size portions that are one-third the size of those used to create the nuts.

7. Roll the portions into balls and flatten the balls into disks.

8. Place one disk at a time in the center of the foam shaping mat. With the double-ended ball tool, rub the disk in a circular motion to thin and curl it to the width needed to cover the head of a nut. **Expert option:** omit the foam shaping mat. Instead use the palm of a hand.

9. Place the caps on an inverted silicone cell former so that they hold their convex shape.

10. With the blade of a craft utility knife, etch a diamond crosshatch on each cap.

11. Set the caps aside for at least one hour to firm up before handling again.

12. Assemble the acorns by placing the caps on the blunt ends of the nuts. Curl them around the heads of the nuts so that they fit snugly.

13. With a toothpick or pointed sculpting implement, bore a small hole in the center of each acorn's cap to fit a stem.

14. To make stems, roll a small ball of bittersweet modeling chocolate into a ⅛-inch (3 mm) thick rope. With a craft utility knife, trim off ½-inch (13 mm) long portions.

15. Fit the stems into the holes of the caps and twist them to secure.

16. Dust the acorns lightly with gold luster dust for sheen.

17. Finish them with a light dusting of cocoa powder for earthiness.

Marbling

This majestic wedding cake was designed for a wedding whose colors were royal blue, silver, and white. The couple requested a square cake with a bold marble pattern and blue fabric bows. For this cake, I used two modeling chocolate techniques: the swirled marble effect and the paneling method.

Note: It is extremely important that all of the modeling chocolate colors be of the same consistency when executing this method or the chocolate will not blend effectively.

Linear Marble Effect

This technique yields a marble with striations that run in only one direction. It works well for creating linear movement, such as the window reflections on a moving car.

Items Needed

- Two or more contrasting colors of modeling chocolate
- Rolled modeling chocolate equipment (page 29)

1. Begin by kneading two colors of modeling chocolate (separately) until they have a pliable and like consistency. Roll out equal length cords of each color into 8-12 inch (20-30 cm) ropes.

2. Twist the two colors together.

3. Roll the twist into one seamless rope that is at least 12 inches (30 cm) long.

4. Fold the rope in half and twist again…

…and again…

…and again.

5. Roll, fold, twist, and repeat 3–5 more times until the tones are well intertwined. The more twists and folds of the rope, the more subtle the marble effect will be. Too many twists and folds will cause the colors to blend into one.

6. Once the desired level of blend is achieved, condense the folded rope into a rectangular shape.

7. Using the palm of a hand, flatten the rope into a seamless patty.

8. Using a silicone rolling pin, roll the patty between two pieces of parchment paper until the desired thinness is achieved. **Expert option:** roll the patty through a commercial sheeter. The pasta machine is not recommended for this method.

◀ Mixing two primary colors such as red and yellow results in a marble that appears orange.

▶ Three or more contrasting tones yield an even busier effect.

Swirled Marble Effect

This technique yields a marble that stirs with movement. It is particularly apt for sky, water, and cork effects.

1. Begin by kneading two colors of modeling chocolate (separately) until they have a pliable and like consistency. Roll them into equal-length cords.

2. Proceed with Steps 2–5 of the Linear Marble Effect.

3. Once the desired depth of marble is achieved, roll the twisted rope out into one uniform 12-inch (30 cm) rope.

4. Twist the uniform rope into a tight S shape. Fit two or more S's together if large sheets are needed.

5. Using the palm of a hand, flatten the S into a seamless patty.

6. Roll the S by hand between two pieces of parchment paper until the desired thickness is achieved. Proceed with Steps 4–9 of Rolling by Hand (page 35).

Wood Grain Effect

1. Begin by kneading bittersweet and white modeling chocolate (separately) until they have a pliable and like consistency. Roll them into equal-length cords.

2. Proceed with Steps 2–5 of the Linear Marble Effect. (see page 83)

3. When the desired depth of wood grain is achieved, flatten the twisted rope into one 12-inch (30 cm) rope.

4. Twist the rope into itself like a snail.

5. Using the palm of a hand, flatten the snail into a seamless patty.

6. Roll the patty by hand between pieces of parchment paper until desired thickness is achieved. Proceed with Steps 4–9 of Rolling by Hand (page 35).

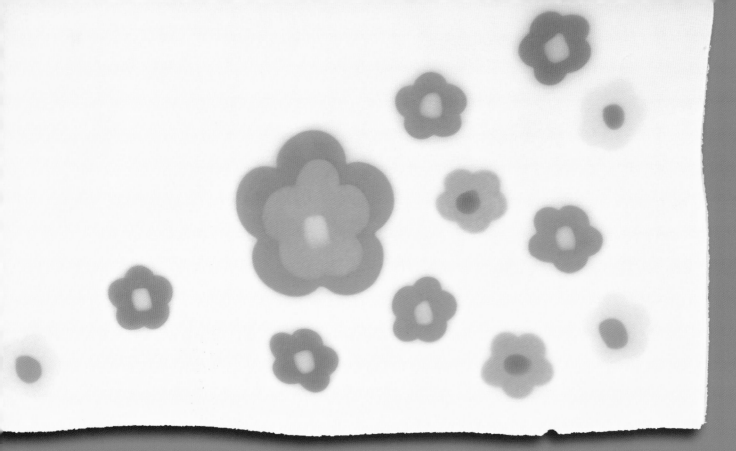

Pattern Inlay Effects

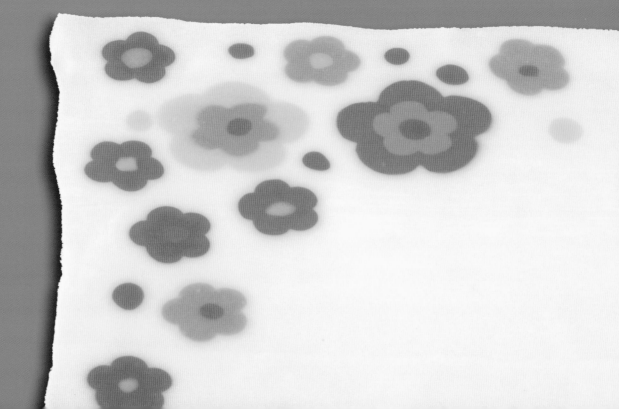

Flower Blossoms

Here, red flower blossoms are seamlessly laid into a rolled modeling chocolate wrap on an 8-inch (20 cm) diameter, 4-inch (10 cm) tall cake.

Items Needed

- Flexible measuring tape
- Red and white modeling chocolate
- Rolled modeling chocolate equipment (page 29)
- Assorted plunger cutters or small blossom cutters
- Fondant smoother
- Parchment paper cone filled with vanilla buttercream

1. Begin by measuring the cake to be wrapped. In this case, one 26x5-inch (66x13 cm) panel is required with the extra inch (25 mm) added all around for insurance.

2. Roll the panels of white modeling chocolate out to ⅛-inch (3 mm) thickness. Cover them with plastic wrap and set them aside.

3. Mix small amounts of dark red modeling chocolate with small amounts of white modeling chocolate to create a second, lighter red hue. Roll the red hues into ¹⁄₁₆-inch (1.6 mm) thick sheets.

4. Using assorted small blossom cutters, cut flowers of different sizes from the red tones. Arrange them in clusters at the corners of each white chocolate sheet. Space the flowers at least ⅓-inch (8 mm) apart, as they will expand when rolled.

5. Lay a piece of parchment paper on the top of the decorated sheets and press down with the pad of the thumb on top of each flower to fuse them into place.

6. With a silicone rolling pin, roll gently over the parchment to fully inlay the design. Roll in multiple directions so that the flowers spread evenly. Feel the surface of the chocolate to check for any parts that are still raised. Rub over any raised parts with a fondant smoother.

7. Allow the chocolate to set for 30–60 minutes before attempting to peel the parchment paper away.

8. Affix the sheets to the cake using the Paneling Method (page 39).

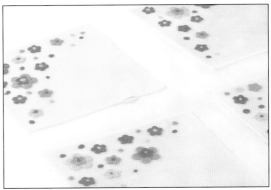

9. Dot the center of some of the flowers with butter cream to finish.

Note Flowers can also be inlaid over one another for the groovy wallpaper effect shown to the left in the close-up of a Hawaiian-themed wedding cake. Proceed as per the Flower Blossom Inlay Effect but stack different colored buds on top of one another. Press a small ball of modeling chocolate into the center of each one and dot more balls of modeling chocolate around the flower pattern for a confetti effect.

Leopard Print

This cake was for a birthday girl whose favorite thing ever is leopard print shoes. It is comprised of 5x5x4-inch (13x13x10 cm) and 9x9x4-inch (23x23x10 cm) square tiers that are tapered out. Exactly two inches (5 cm) of cake is shaved off the diameter of each tier's base. The cake is wrapped in rolled modeling chocolate using the Paneling Method (page 39).

Items Needed

- White, yellow, orange, bittersweet, and tan modeling chocolate
- Rolled modeling chocolate equipment (page 29)
- Small round plunger cutters, ¾, ½, ⅓, and ⅛-inch (19, 13, 8, and 3 mm) in diameter

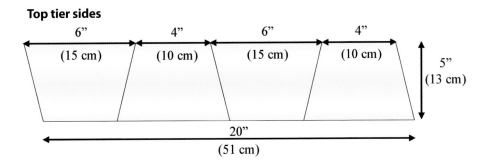

Top tier sides

6"	4"	6"	4"
(15 cm)	(10 cm)	(15 cm)	(10 cm)

5"
(13 cm)

20"
(51 cm)

Bottom tier sides

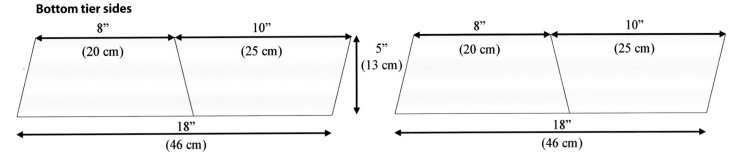

8"	10"
(20 cm)	(25 cm)

5"
(13 cm)

18"
(46 cm)

8"	10"
(20 cm)	(25 cm)

18"
(46 cm)

1. First, measure the dimensions of the sides of the cake to be covered in leopard print panels. In this case, the eight sides are isosceles trapezoids whose tops are 2 inches (50 mm) wider than their bottoms, as shown below. As per the Paneling Method, factor an extra inch (25 mm) into the measurements of each piece for insurance.

2. Marble white and yellow modeling chocolate using the Linear Marble Effect (page 83).

3. Using the measurements above, create three sheets of rolled modeling chocolate. Roll them to ⅛-inch (3 mm) thickness.

4. Roll out the orange, tan, and bittersweet modeling chocolate into ¹⁄₁₆-inch (1.6 mm) thick sheets.

5. Using the ¾- and ½-inch (19 and 13 mm) plunger cutters, cut orange circles of rolled modeling chocolate and place them haphazardly on the white/yellow marbled sheets, spaced ½-inch (13 mm) apart.

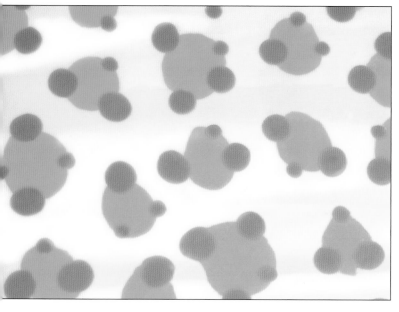

6. With a silicone rolling pin, roll the chocolate gently by hand between pieces of parchment paper to blend until the spots are inlaid.

7. Using the ⅓- and ⅛-inch (8 and 3 mm) plunger cutters, cut tan circles of rolled modeling chocolate and cluster them around the edges of the orange spots.

8. With a silicone rolling pin, roll the chocolate gently between pieces of parchment paper to blend until the spots are inlaid.

9. Using the ⅓-inch (8 mm) plunger cutter, cut bittersweet circles of rolled modeling chocolate and cluster them between the tan spots. Roll again to inlay. **Expert Option:** Apply the spots together and roll them only once to inlay.

10. Cut the panels to size and apply them to the sides of the cake using the Paneling Method (page 39).

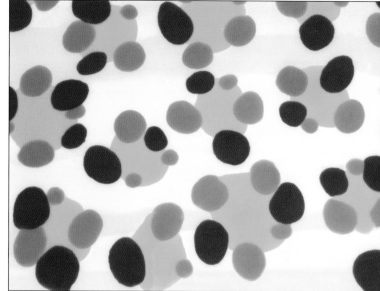

Stripes, Zebra Print & Bubble Print

This baby shower tower was designed for my dear friend, Larisse. We did not know the sex of the baby at the time of her shower, hence the neutral gender theme. The four-tiered design is comprised of the following vanilla buttercream-coated cakes:

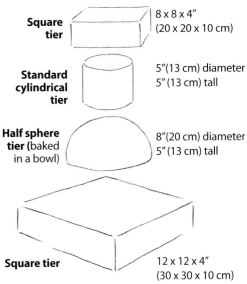

Square tier
8 x 8 x 4"
(20 x 20 x 10 cm)

Standard cylindrical tier
5"(13 cm) diameter
5" (13 cm) tall

Half sphere tier (baked in a bowl)
8"(20 cm) diameter
5" (13 cm) tall

Square tier
12 x 12 x 4"
(30 x 30 x 10 cm)

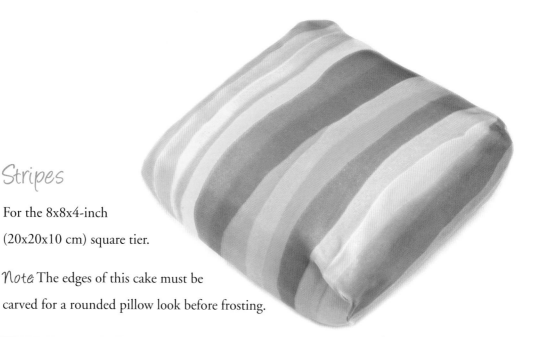

Stripes

For the 8x8x4-inch (20x20x10 cm) square tier.

Note The edges of this cake must be carved for a rounded pillow look before frosting.

Items Needed

- White and pastel yellow, pink, blue, green, and purple modeling chocolate
- Rolled modeling chocolate equipment (page 29)

1. Roll out the white modeling chocolate to $\frac{1}{16}$-inch (1.6 mm) thickness. Create a sheet that is "+" shaped and approximately 13 inches (33 cm) in length, with each extension approximately 8 inches (20 cm) wide. Cover it with plastic wrap when not in use.

2. Roll out the colored modeling chocolate to $\frac{1}{16}$-inch (1.6 mm) thickness.

3. With roller cutter, slice the pastel colors into strips that are anywhere between $\frac{1}{4}$–1 inch (6–25 mm) thick.

4. Cover the white sheet with the strips, overlapping them by $\frac{1}{8}$ inch (3 mm).

5. Roll it between pieces of parchment paper to blend the pattern into one seamless sheet.

6. To cover the pillow, tuck the arms of the "+" under the cake and trim any bulky excess with a craft utility knife.

Zebra Print

For the 5-inch (13 cm) diameter, 5-inch (13 cm) tall standard cylindrical tier.

Items Needed

- White and pastel yellow, pink, blue, green, and purple modeling chocolate
- Rolled modeling chocolate equipment (page 29)

1. Roll out white modeling chocolate to ⅛-inch (3 mm) thickness.

2. Create a sheet that is approximately 17x6 inches (43 x 15 cm) with the extra inch (25 mm) all around for insurance. Cover it with plastic wrap when not in use.

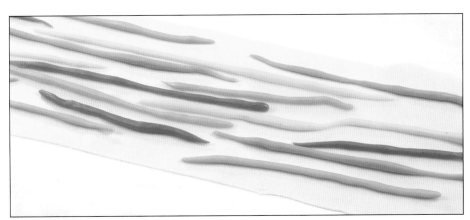

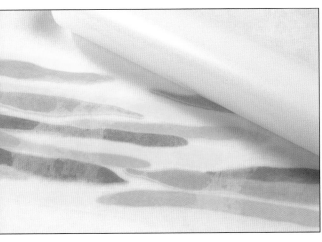

3. Roll out ⅛-inch (3 mm) thin ropes of the pastel colors. Place them horizontally but otherwise haphazardly onto the white sheet, spacing them ¼–½-inch (6–13 mm) apart.

4. With a silicone rolling pin, roll the sheet by hand between pieces of parchment paper until the colors have merged with the backdrop. Roll in multiple directions so that the sheet maintains its original proportions.

5. Allow the sheet to rest for 30–60 minutes before wrapping the cake using the Paneling Method (page 39).

6. Seal the cake in plastic wrap and return it to the refrigerator.

Bubble Print

For the 8-inch (20 cm) diameter, 5-inch (13 cm) tall half sphere tier.

Note Before frosting, the top of this cake must be leveled just enough so that the 5-inch (13 cm) cylindrical tier that sits atop it can sit flush.

1. Roll out a 13-inch (33 cm) circle of white modeling chocolate to ⅛-inch thickness. Cover it with plastic wrap when not in use.

2. Roll the pastel colors out to 1/16-inch (1.6 mm) thickness.

3. Using the round cutters, cut different size circles from the pastel colors and arrange them haphazardly on the white circle. In some cases, pile different colors on top of one another.

4. With a silicone rolling pin, roll the sheet between pieces of parchment paper until it is seamless. Set the piece aside to rest for 10–20 minutes until it is just firm enough to handle. Do not allow the skirt to dry for too long or it will not drape as effectively over the cake; the chocolate must be soft and fresh for this technique to work.

5. Peel the parchment from the chocolate and trim the rough edges.

6. Rub a spoon in an outward direction over the edges of the circle to thin them.

7. Using a blush brush, lightly brush the surface of the chocolate with white sparkle for a silky effect.

8. Drape the chocolate loosely over the sphere cake and arrange it like a skirt, pinching and pleating to achieve a flowing look.

9. Cover the cake loosely with plastic wrap and return it to the refrigerator.

Baby Blocks

For the 12x12x4-inch (30x30x10 cm) square tier

1. For each baby block, cut four strips of pastel-colored rolled modeling chocolate ⅛-inch (3 mm) thick, 3⅔-inches long, and ⅔-inch wide (92x16 mm).

2. Cut a ⅛-inch (3 mm) thick, 4x4-inch (10x10 cm) square of white rolled modeling chocolate.

3. Arrange the colored strips on top of it.

4. Finish with baby-themed molded chocolates.

5. Secure any loose pieces with a dab of melted white chocolate.

To make the pearl ball decorations, roll small hunks of pastel-colored modeling chocolate between two palms. Using a blush brush, dust them with pearl dust to add an iridescent sheen.

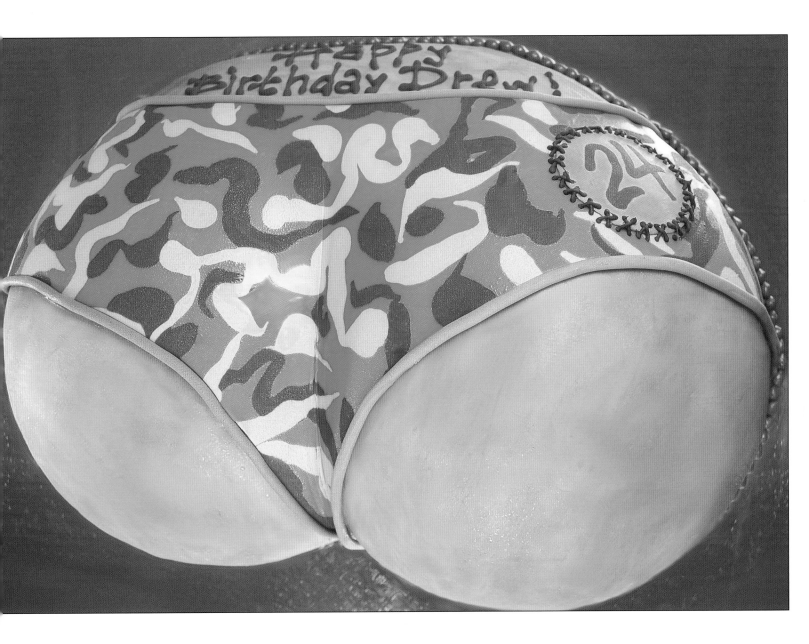

Camouflage

A client from Texas commissioned me to make a booty cake for her son, who was stationed at the naval base in San Diego. Most people don't have a broad lexicon for under-the-pants stuff, so when it comes to fornicakes, I am usually obliged to interpret euphemisms and fill in the blanks where their sentences trail off until we come to a polite agreement over the size and skin tone of … you know. However, this particular woman had a vocabulary so advanced and kinky that I could hardly keep up.

"So do ya vejazzle?" she asked me.

I had no idea what she was talking about. Quick fingers on the keyboard revealed that the term, coined by Jennifer Love Hewitt, means "to accessorize the pooch with jewels." Really considering the notion of bedazzling my own vajayjay led me to wonder out loud how a vejazzler avoids the obvious pitfall of losing a jewel, like, up there, and if this were to tragically happen, what kind of damage control would then ensue.

"Hon!" she said. "I meant have ya ever bedazzled a vajayjay *cake*."

The answer was no, because evidently when it comes to fornicakes, I am a plain vajayjane.

She ordered a Kim Kardashian booty cake with camouflage boy shorts. "And when ya deliver the cake," she added, "say, 'Happy B-day Drew! Here's what yo mama's booty looked like before she had you!'"

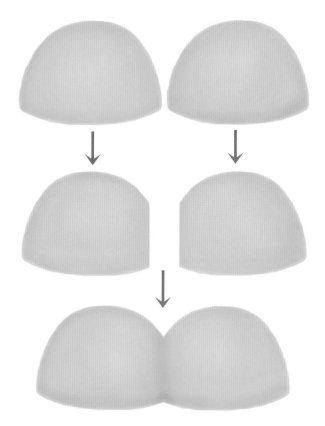

How to Form Butt Cheeks

To form a booty cake, begin with two 8-inch (20 cm) half-sphere cakes baked in 8-inch (20 cm) bowl molds.

Slice approximately 15 percent off one side of each half-sphere, then sandwich them together at the seam. Reincorporate the trimmed cake parts over the seam on one side to form a small lower back. Coat the booty with flesh-colored buttercream.

Camouflage Boy Shorts

1. With flexible measuring tape, calculate the width of the waist by measuring the distance on the cake from hip to hip. Also measure the distance the long way from the waistband to the cake platter to calculate the length of thong needed. In this case, the waistband must be at least 18 inches (46 cm) wide and the thong must be at least 7 inches (18 cm) long.

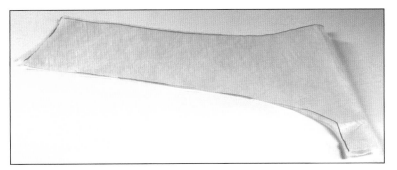

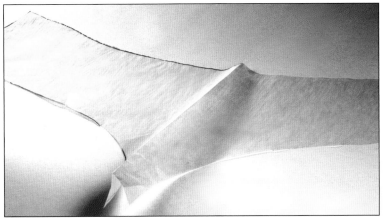

2. Trace a template for the boy shorts out of a full sheet of parchment paper. Create a 19-inch (48 cm) waistband and an 8-inch (20 cm) thong, which includes an extra inch (25 mm) for insurance. Use the fold and cut technique so that the sides are symmetrical. Fit the template around the cake to make sure it is the right length, shape, and snugness for the booty. Trim it with scissors as needed.

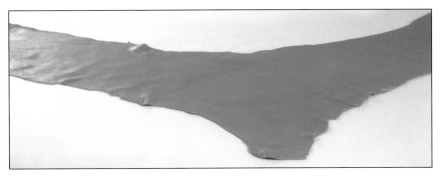

3. Roll out sheets of green modeling chocolate to ⅛-inch (3 mm).

4. Patch them together in the shape of the boy shorts using the parchment template as guide.

5. Roll the shorts between two pieces of parchment paper to bind any loose seams. Cover them with plastic wrap when not in use.

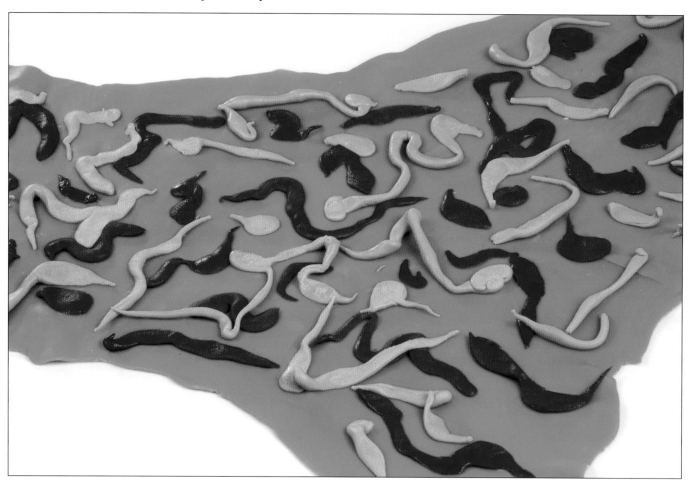

6. By hand, roll ¹⁄₁₆–⅛-inch (1.6–3 mm) diameter thick ropes of bittersweet and tan modeling chocolate. Distribute them evenly but in a haphazard configuration over the surface of the shorts, overlapping them in some places.

7. Place a piece of parchment paper on top of the design and roll it with a silicone rolling pin until the chocolate is seamless.

8. Since the chocolate will have stretched from rolling, trim the boy shorts back down to size using the parchment template. Slide them onto the cake and position them squarely into place. Trim any overhang at the hip with a craft utility knife.

9. Combine the scraps and knead them together to yield army green color. Extrude that through the 1 cm round die of a clay extruder gun to make ribbing. Place the ribbing around the hem to complete the shorts.

Word/Number Inlay

Those who grew up in the 80s may remember the odd character, Sloth from the movie, Goonies, the deformed and friendly monster whose signature line is, "Hey you guys!" This is an example of how numbers or words can be inlaid in rolled modeling chocolate to make captions or inscriptions. In this example, the font is designed to look loony like Sloth's voice.

Items Needed

- Red and white modeling chocolate
- Rolled modeling chocolate equipment (page 29)
- Clay extruder with 1 mm diameter round die
- Cocoa powder
- Small paintbrush

1. Roll out a small sheet of white modeling chocolate to ⅛-inch (3 mm) thickness and trim it to a size that is roughly 1 inch (25 mm) larger in shape than the one desired for the word bubble.

2. Push red modeling chocolate through a clay extruder fitted with a 1 mm diameter die to create thin strings.

3. With a craft utility knife, cut the strings to form letters. Arrange the letters on top of the white rolled modeling chocolate to complete the words.

4. Roll the sheet between two pieces of parchment to inlay the letters.

5. Trim around the edges with a craft utility knife to form the shape of a word bubble.

6. Using the small paintbrush, brush the edges with cocoa powder to accentuate the bubble's outline.

7. Allow the word bubble to firm up on parchment paper for at least 1 hour before placing it on the side of a cake.

8. Position the bubble so that some of the edges surpass the cake's boundaries in the same way that a word bubble sometimes exceeds the edges of a comic strip.

Figurines
& Creatures

Heads, Limbs & Bodies

Note This technique requires non-edible infrastructure for support. The infrastructure may be omitted but then the structural integrity of the figurines will be more at risk.

Items Needed

- White, flesh, pink, and bittersweet modeling chocolate
- Rolled modeling chocolate equipment (page 29)
- Styrofoam ball, 1-inch (25 mm) diameter
- 2 lollypop sticks
- Piece of styrofoam
- Ball tool
- Blunt sculpting implement
- Pointed sculpting implement
- Flat sculpting implement
- Round cutter, 1½-inch (38 mm) diameter
- Round cutter, 1 cm diameter
- Parchment paper cone filled with dark chocolate

Heads & Faces

This modeling chocolate cake topper was designed for the birthday of a boy whose party involved tubing. He also happens to look just like Harry Potter himself, so this is a dual-meaning interpretation of the birthday boy floating into another year of life with buttercream frosting lapping at his knees.

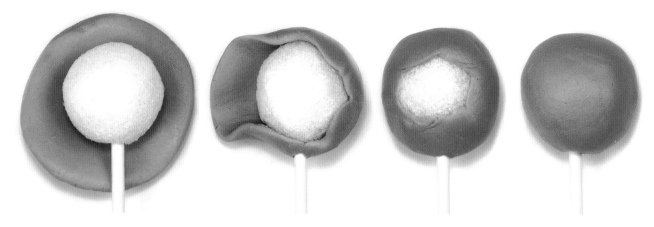

1. Press a lollypop stick halfway into a styrofoam ball to form a neck-head connection.

2. Flatten a small marble of flesh-colored modeling chocolate into a ¼-inch (6 mm) thick, 2-inch diameter (50 mm) disk.

3. Wrap the disk around the styrofoam ball. The back of the head may remain bare (unless a bald head is desired), as it will eventually be concealed by hair anyway. The front of the head must maintain a thick enough layer to sculpt into a face. From here on out, handle the head only by the lollypop stick. When not in use, keep it skewered on a piece of styrofoam separate from the body.

4. To form a nose, roll a blunt sculpting implement in a V-shape in the center of the face, pushing the modeling chocolate into a small mound.

5. To form eyes sockets, press the large end of a ball tool into the face on either side of the nose.

6. Imprint a smile by pressing the curved edge of the 1½-inch (38 mm) diameter round cutter into the space beneath the nose.

7. To create irises, roll a small piece of white modeling chocolate out to ¹⁄₁₆-inch (1.6 mm) thickness.

8. Cut two small circles using the 1 cm diameter round cutter. Release them from the cutter using the tip of a blunt implement.

 9. Press the white circles into the center of the eye sockets.

10. Melt dark chocolate in the microwave, oven, or over a hot water bath.

11. Dip the tip of a pointed sculpting implement into the melted chocolate and dab the center of each eyeball to form pupils.

12. Add any desired details such as glasses, eyelashes, rouge, or lipstick at this stage.

Short Hair

1. Fill a parchment paper cone with melted chocolate and pipe it onto the back of the head and around the face to create hair. Allow it to dry.

2. Pipe a second layer of hair on top of the first to add volume and a layered look.

Long Hair

1. Roll bittersweet (or desired color) of modeling chocolate out to 1/16-inch (1.6 mm) thickness.

2. Cut it into a 3-inch (76 mm) wide half-moon shape. Place the head (still on the stick) in the middle of the half moon.

3. Using a craft utility knife, cut a wavy edge around the half moon to give the hair body. Cut a V-shape out of the top so that the hair can bend easier around the head.

4. From behind, press the hair onto the back of the head to secure it. Add a drop of water if needed to act as glue.

5. Fit the hair around the forehead for bangs, pressing it into the scalp in some places, then curling it outwards in other places. Leave the remainder of the hair loose and flowing down the back. Trim if necessary.

6. Allow the figurine to set for at least 1 hour or ideally overnight before handling it again.

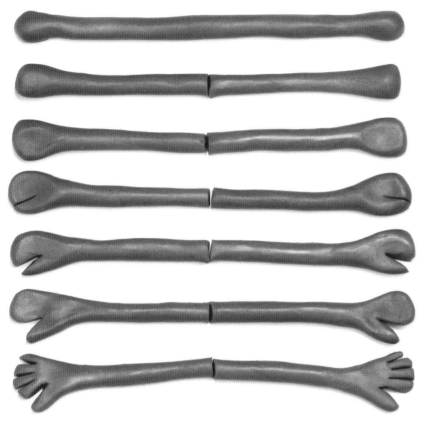

Arms, Hands & Fingers

1. For one set of arms with hands, roll out a rope of modeling chocolate with teardrop-shaped ends. Cut it down the middle to create two equal-length arms.

2. With the pad of a finger, flatten the teardrop ends gently.

3. With a craft utility knife, slice one-third of the way through the tips of each hand to make mirroring thumbs.

4. With the flat sculpting implement, round the sharp edges. Stop at this stage if mitten hands are desired.

5. Cut three slices to make four fingers. Cut so that the pinkies are slightly smaller than the other three fingers.

6. With the flat sculpting implement, separate the fingers and gently round their tips.

7. Set the arms aside for 10–30 minutes to set before handling again.

Legs & Feet

Note: The legs and feet shown here are sculpted for a backside view for a swimmer or person kneeling.

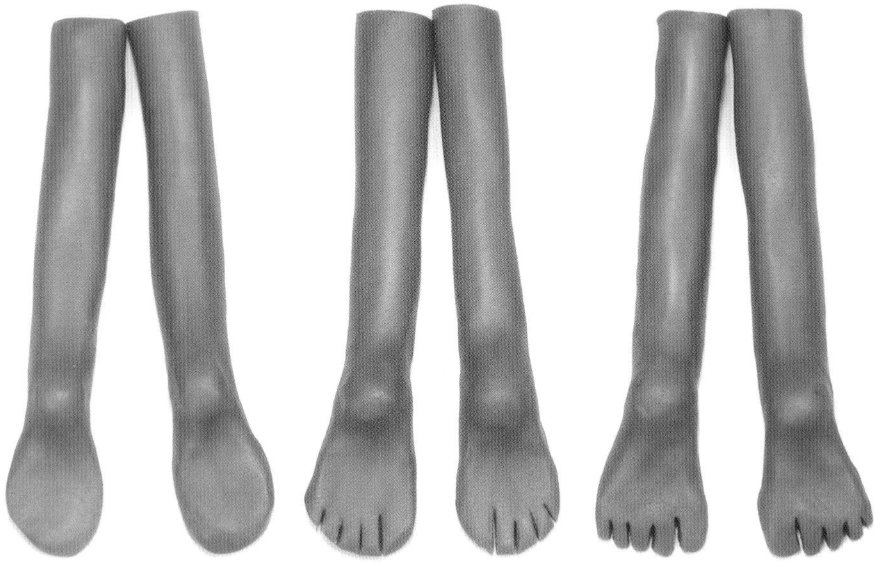

1. For one set of legs with feet, begin as per the arms by rolling out a rope of modeling chocolate with teardrop-shaped ends. Cut it in the middle to create two equal-length legs.

2. With the pad of a finger, flatten the teardrop ends gently.

3. With a ball tool, shape heels. Cover the feet with shoes at this point if desired.

4. To form toes, slice four times across the top of the foot with a craft utility knife. Slice them so that they shrink in size from the big toe to the pinkie.

5. With the flat sculpting implement, separate the toes. Gently round their tips.

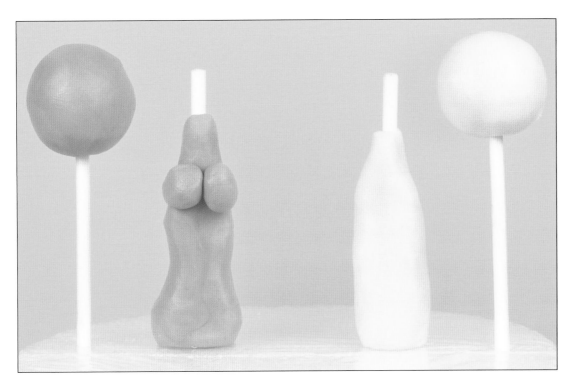

Bodies

1. Begin with a lollypop stick anchored into a piece of styrofoam. Orient the body on the styrofoam as it is intended to sit on the cake.

2. Roll out a log of flesh-colored modeling chocolate and skewer it on the lollypop stick the long way down the middle.

3. Shape the log into a body that narrows at the neck. Leave just enough bare lollypop stick at the top to accommodate the head. For male figurines (above right), create boxy torsos. For female figurines (above left), create curvy torsos with narrowed waists and wider hips. Add breasts by pressing two small balls of modeling chocolate into the chest.

4. Before dressing a figurine, check its proportions by assembling the limbs loosely on the torso. Pin the legs beneath the torso. Affix the arms at the shoulders. Trim limbs or make any necessary adjustments if needed at this stage.

To render a crouching effect, bend the legs underneath the torso.

Clothes

The trick to dressing figurines is to make parts like sleeves and pant legs separately. All the clothes here are made from 1/16-inch (1.6 mm) rolled modeling chocolate.

To make short sleeves, cut two-third moons out of rolled modeling chocolate and wrap them around the tops of the arms, folding all seams to the back.

To make long sleeves, cut long narrow rectangles of rolled modeling chocolate and wrap them around the arms, facing the seam to the back.

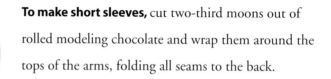

To create basic shirts, cut a rectangle of rolled modeling chocolate. Cut three half-moons symmetrically across the top.

Place the torso piece face down in the middle of the shirt. Fold the flaps around the back and over the shoulders. Roll a blunt sculpting implement over the seams to flatten.

To affix arms to a torso, dab the shoulders with a drop of water and attach sleeves seam-side down. Use a pointed sculpting implement to smooth over seams.

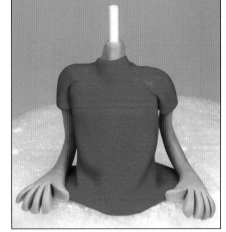

To create a basic dress, cut a half-moon shape out of rolled modeling chocolate.

Fold it like an inverted cone over the body. Cut down the middle of the back to create a straight seam then pull away the excess. With a craft utility knife, trim around the top to create a neckline. Attach sleeves.

To create a suit, cut a collar and lapels and fold them around the front of the torso to meet so that the seam runs visibly down the front of the chest.

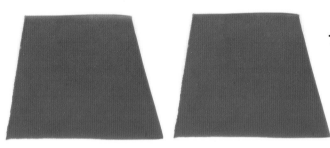

To create shorts, cut trapezoids and roll them into open cones with the larger openings facing the knees.

Insert the legs into the cones and press down at the back to secure them. Pin the back of the legs underneath the torso. For pant legs, create longer pieces that cover the entire leg.

Zen and the Art of a Koi Cake

This Koi Cake was created for a wedding that took place in the Japanese Friendship Garden in California's Balboa Park, an outdoor venue under a canopy of trees with winding paths, gurgling water, crooked bonsai, a Zen rock garden, and a pond full of plump, spotted koi. The groom requested a tangerine-colored fish made of red velvet cake with pink cream cheese frosting so that when sliced, it would look like sashimi inside.

The average fish has over one thousand tiny scales on its body. In comparison, this cake is covered with roughly 200 modeling chocolate circles. The circles are placed on the cake from the bottom up, like shingles. It's tedious work, but the result is a colorful and artistic dessert.

Items Needed

- ½ sheet cake, 4 inches (10 cm) in height to form the fish body
- 4 cups of buttercream (see recipe, page 149) for crumb coating
- Modeling chocolate equipment (page 29)
- ½ sheet cardboard for support
- Glue dots or hot glue to affix cardboard to Plexiglas
- White, light orange, dark orange, red, and black modeling chocolate
- Spoon
- Super pearl dust
- Orange and yellow luster dust
- Small paint brush
- ¾-inch (19 mm) diameter round cutter
- Pointed sculpting implement
- Piping bag full of melted white chocolate for piping garnish on scales

1. Precut a 16-inch (41 cm) long piece of double cardboard in a plump "S" formation to serve both as a guideline for carving and to support the belly of the fish throughout production.

2. Cut the ½ sheet cake in half the long way. Stack it on top of itself to double its height. Then carve the cake into an undulating fish shape. Cover the carved cake with plastic wrap and press the cake with an open hand to condense the loose parts and help mold the desired shape. Refrigerate the cake for at least one hour.

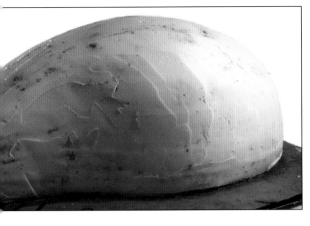

3. Crumb coat the fish body with buttercream and place it in the refrigerator for at least one hour to harden.

4. Roll the light orange, dark orange, red and some of the white modeling chocolate to a thickness of ¹⁄₁₆-inch (1.6 mm). With a ¾-inch (19 mm) diameter round cutter, cut 200 uniform circles. Set them aside.

5. Create eyeballs by flattening out two small balls of white modeling chocolate with the palm of a hand. Create pupils by flattening smaller balls of black modeling chocolate. Affix the pupils to the center of the eyeballs using a dab of water.

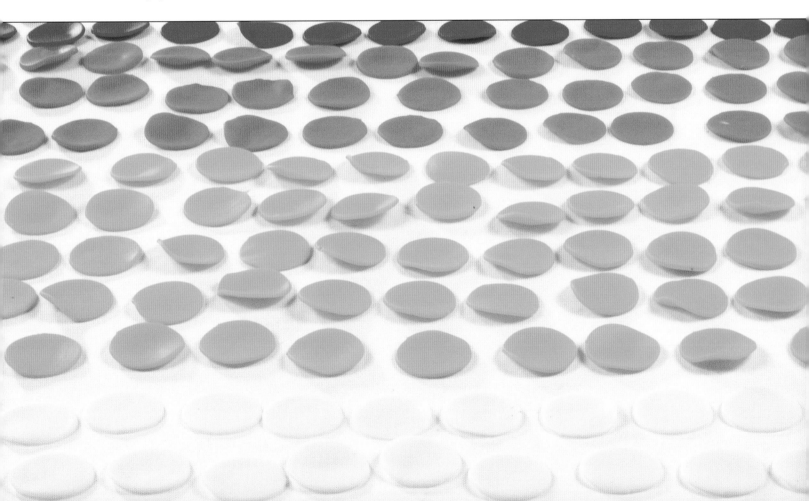

6. Form lips by rolling out two ropes of white modeling chocolate with tapered ends.

7. Brush the lips and eyeballs with super pearl dust, then rub them with the pad of the thumb to make their surfaces smooth and shiny.

8. Roll out sheets of ⅛-inch (4 mm) thick white modeling chocolate and cut them into fins. Create two long pieces to make a rear caudal fin, two squarish pieces to make the left and right pelvic fins, two rounded pieces to make the left and right pectoral fins, and one long piece the length of the cake to create a dorsal fin. Thin the ends of each fin by rubbing the back of a spoon over their edges until the modeling chocolate is so fine that it begins to shred. With a pointed implement, etch rays into the fins to create a ribbed texture. With a small paintbrush, paint the narrower ends of the fins with orange and yellow luster dust. Brush over them again with super pearl dust to add an iridescent sheen.

9. Attach the chocolate elements of the caudal fin to the tail of the cake and bend them around the platter in a "U" shape.

10. Add one row of half scales around the entire base of the cake to conceal the crumb coat.

11. Beginning at the tail, lay the circles overlapping like shingles. Lay them starting at the bottom of the cake and working up only, one row at a time, from back to front. Cluster like colors to create a patchy, spotted effect. Where the gills of a fish would be, add a "U" of red circles. Eventually the scales will meet at the fish's nose.

12. Cover the seam that runs along the top with the dorsal fin.

13. Attach the eyes and lips to the cake using a dab of melted white chocolate as glue. Place the pelvic and pectoral fins at the base of the cake accordingly.

14. Pipe trim on every scale using melted white chocolate. Pipe around the lips as well.

Happy as a Pig in ... Chocolate!

This lovable Pig Cake was designed for the wedding reception of a couple of pig knickknack collectors and the proud parents of a real live oinker by the name of Luke Skywalker.

For a cake artist, the challenge of rendering creatures involves striking a balance between alive and yummy. The goal is to provide a generous enough dose of realism to accurately convey the animal while maintaining a sweet and appealing aesthetic that is still mindful of a dessert. Making it look good enough to eat is a matter of putting one's self in the cake's hooves, then imagining how the world would look if it were all made of dessert.

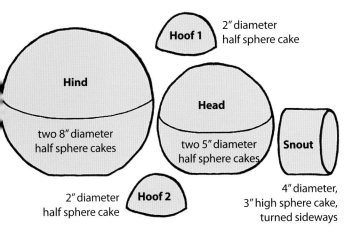

Hoof 1 — 2" diameter half sphere cake

Hind — two 8" diameter half sphere cakes

Head — two 5" diameter half sphere cakes

Snout

2" diameter half sphere cake — Hoof 2

4" diameter, 3" high sphere cake, turned sideways

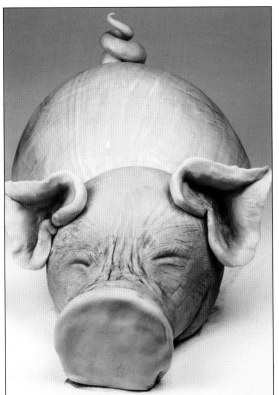

It's easier to make the parts of an animal's body individually than it is to carve, frost, and cover one continuous shape, so in this case, the head, hind, and two front hooves are each different cakes that are assembled after decorating.

The whole cake is comprised of six half-sphere shapes for the body parts and one cylinder cake for the snout. The two larger sets of half-spheres are combined to create full spheres for the hind and head parts. Each one is then slightly truncated on the bottom to prevent rolling.

Spherical cakes are best baked in bowls to minimize the amount of carving that is needed.

What helps piggy look realistic is his hide, which is a 50:50 combination of modeling chocolate and fondant that is etched with the tines of a fork then dusted with cocoa powder and pink luster dust for a fur effect. The 50 percent fondant adds the elasticity that is needed to cover such highly contoured shapes. The 50 percent modeling chocolate permits a level of sculpting and texturing that makes the features come to life.

Items Needed

- Two large half-sphere cakes, 8-inch (20 cm) diameter, for the body
- Two medium half-sphere cakes, 5-inch (13 cm) diameter, for the head
- Two small half-sphere or egg-shaped cakes, 2-inch (5 cm) diameter, for the hooves
- One 4-inch (10 cm) diameter, 3-inch (8 cm) high cylinder cake (standard round) for the snout
- Vanilla buttercream for frosting (recipe, pg. 150)
- Rubber glove
- White modeling chocolate
- Equal amount of fondant
- Pink and brown gel food color
- Modeling chocolate equipment (page 29)
- Pink luster dust
- Plastic wrap
- Fork
- Blunt sculpting implement
- Cocoa powder
- 1½ cups chocolate glaze (see Wicked Goodies website for recipe)
- Chocolate buttercream, for the mud puddle (recipe, page 153)

1. Truncate the head and the hind cakes on the bottom slightly so that they sit without rolling.

2. Carve one sliver off the side of the head to accommodate the back of the snout.

3. Carve the hooves into egg shapes. Carve a wedge into the middle of each hoof to distinguish the two big toes that characterize pig feet.

4. Hollow out shallow sockets in the hind to fit the hooves and head later on.

5. Crumb coat each part of the cake with buttercream. Use the cupped palm of a gloved hand to smooth the frosting into a rounded shape. Store the parts separately in the refrigerator, wrapped in plastic when not in use.

6. Combine one part white modeling chocolate and one part white fondant with pink and brown food coloring. Knead them all together until a pig skin-tone is achieved.

7. Roll out the mixture to a thickness of approximately ⅛-inch (4 mm) and begin covering each part of the cake using the Draping Method (page 42). When covering the head, bunch the extra skin around the snout and pinch the brow to create wrinkles.

8. For the rest of the body parts, pull and smooth the skin over each piece of cake, tucking any seams into the places that will be concealed once the pig is assembled, i.e. the back of the head, the neck, and the hoof orbits. Keep all the pieces sealed in plastic wrap when not in use.

9. On the head and hind, etch gently on top of the plastic wrap with the tines of a fork to create the effect of wrinkles and hairs. Brush in different directions to add texture.

10. Use a blunt modeling instrument to add shape and character to the eyes, snout, and jowls.

11. Remove the plastic wrap and brush the cake lightly with cocoa powder to weather the skin and accentuate the details. Buff again with pink luster dust to add a natural blush.

12. Using a blunt modeling instrument, bore nostrils into the snout.

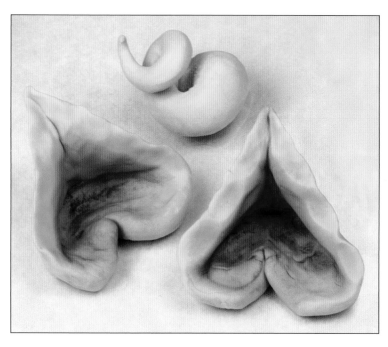

13. Create a corkscrew tail and meaty ears out of the remaining modeling chocolate/fondant. Brush the inside of the ears with cocoa powder to add depth.

14. Affix the ears and tail with dabs of melted white chocolate to the head and hind respectively.

15. Assemble the body parts on the serving platform.

16. Using a small offset spatula, frost the empty space on the serving platform with chocolate buttercream.

17. Garnish the scene as desired with chocolate malt balls, truffles, modeling chocolate roses, and crumbled chocolate "dirt."

18. Drizzle chocolate glaze on top of the cake, especially between the pig's head and hind to conceal the neck seam.

Advanced Engineering: Monuments

The Colosseum, the Parthenon, and the Lighthouse of Alexandria comprise this edible salute to ancient architecture. This wedding cake celebrated the union of Victoria Leonidova-Shtilkind and Yanni Alexander Shainsky. About the choice of cake design, Yanni said:

> Our wedding had a "Greek Mythology & Ancient World" theme. The three different layers each represent the three stages of our joint life together. At the beginning, married couples fight like gladiators in a Colosseum. When their differences are resolved, and they grow to know one another implicitly, they are ready to build something as beautiful and long lasting as the Parthenon, in the form of a family. After many years of love and bliss, we hope that our matrimony will serve as a beacon to the next generation, as represented by the Lighthouse of Alexandria. The cake also symbolizes the youth, middle-aged, and elderly generations that gathered to share our wedding with us.

This design consists of 5 cake tiers and one gingerbread lighthouse. Two of the cake tiers are carved in the shape of mounds, coated in buttercream then covered in cake sand to resemble the dry Mediterranean earth and to allow each monument to stand alone. A network of wooden dowels within the tiers support the weight of the cakes stacked above while thin sharpened dowels hold the tiers in line.

The Colosseum

Items Needed

- 13-inch diameter, 4-inch high round, cold, crumb-coated cake
- Ivory, dark brown, and medium brown modeling chocolate
- Modeling chocolate equipment (page 29)
- ½-inch diameter oval cutter
- Cocoa powder
- Gold luster dust
- Gold leaf
- Clay extruder with ½ cm opening
- ¾-inch (19 mm) square cutter
- ¼, ½, ¾-inch (6, 13, and 19 mm) round cutters
- Paper cones for piping
- Melted white and dark chocolate for piping

1. Roll out the three shades of modeling chocolate and cut three sizes of circles using small round cutters with the diameters ¼, ½, ¾-inch (6, 13, and 19 mm). Use round piping tips in place of cutters if need be. Pile the circles in a nesting formation to create decorative *clipea* (shields) to be affixed later on to the *discriptio* (the top portion of the walls) as per the original look of the outer Colosseum.

2. With the leftover scraps of dark brown, medium brown, and ivory modeling chocolate, roll and twist using the Linear Marble Effect (page 83) to create the semblance of travertine stone.

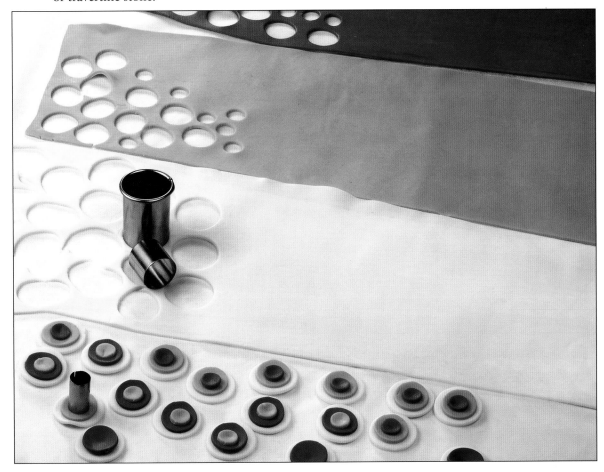

3. Roll out ⅛-inch (3 mm) thin sheets of marbled modeling chocolate to create one 41x4.5-inch (105x 11 cm) slab, as well as one 13.5-inch (34 cm) circle. Proceed to wrap the cake using the Paneling Method (page 39).

4. Combine the excess trim with an equal amount of white modeling chocolate to create a lighter shade of brown marble. Roll it out ¼-inch (6 mm) thick and cut it into small ¾-inch (19 mm) squares.

5. Using an oval cutter, remove the centers to create an archway effect. Set them aside.

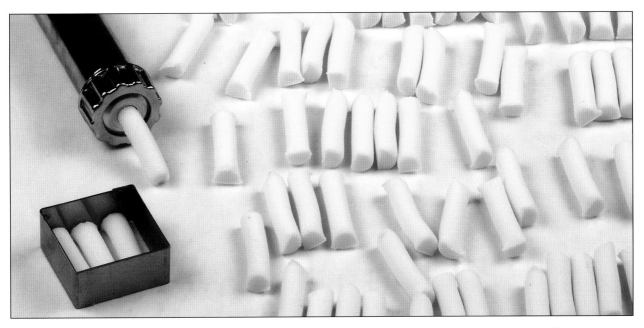

6. Using a clay extruder fitted with a ½ cm round opening, create ropes of ivory modeling chocolate. Cut them into uniform columns using the same square cutter used to create the archways. Set them aside.

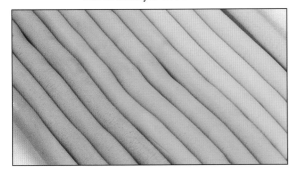

7. With the same die on the extruder, create long ropes of light brown modeling chocolate and set them aside.

8. Begin decorating the Colosseum at its base by alternating archways and columns. Because modeling chocolate is tacky, the small parts should adhere to sides of the cake on contact. Dab the back of any loose decorations with melted chocolate to help them stick.

9. Once the first row is complete, line the top with a rope of light brown modeling chocolate.

10. Proceed with two more rows of archways, columns, and ropes.

11. Prepare a batch of melted white chocolate and dark chocolate and mix ⅓ of each to create a light chocolate shade. Thin out the chocolate if needed with vegetable oil to achieve a good piping consistency, then pipe a capital and base for each column.

12. Add the clipea decorations to the topmost portion of the Colosseum. Use the archways to guide their placement in an every-other formation. With the three tones of piping chocolate, add trim to the archways and detail to the cake's décor. Once the chocolate has set fully, use a small paintbrush to gild selected parts of the piped deco lightly with gold luster dust. Brush the columns with cocoa powder to add depth. Accent the cake's edge with gold leaf to convey a look of opulence. Insert thick dowels to support the weight of cakes above.

The Parthenon

Items Needed

- 12x6x4-inch (30x15x10 cm) rectangle of cake
- 12x3x3-inch (30x8x8 cm) rectangle of cake for the roof
- Five or more 13x7-inch (33x 18 cm) rectangles of cardboard
- Glue dots or hot glue
- White electrical tape
- White modeling chocolate
- Modeling chocolate equipment (page 29)
- 4.5-inch (11 cm) wide triangular silicone heirloom mold
- Melted white and dark chocolate for dipping and piping
- Vegetable oil
- Clay extruder with ½ cm square die
- 40 Pepperidge Farm® Pirouette® Rolled Wafers
- Cocoa powder
- Super pearl dust
- Drinking cup

1. The cardboard base must be ¾-inch (19 mm) thick or sturdy enough to perch without bowing atop the round "mountain" of cake below, which lends support only in the middle. Create the thick base by gluing (with a glue gun, glue dots, or glue) four or more sheets of 13x7-inch (33x18 cm) cardboard together. Rim the rough edges with white electrical tape.

2. Cut the 12x3x3-inch (30x8x8 cm) cake diagonally the long way. Atop one 13x7-inch (33x18 cm) piece of cardboard, create a 3-inch (30 cm) high triangular roof with a 1-inch (25 mm) *frieze* (flat vertical surface on which to later affix *metopes* and pipe *triglyphs*). Hollow out a 6-inch (15 cm) circle in the roof's center to later fit a second hunk of

mountainous terrain. Freeze the roof and the foundation. Crumb coat both elements. Apply a second coating of buttercream, taking care to conceal all evidence of the cake beneath, as any dark spots in the buttercream will show like bruises through the slightly translucent ivory modeling chocolate.

3. With equal parts ivory and white modeling chocolate, twist and fold as per the Swirled Marble Effect (pg. 86). Roll out to a thickness of ⅛-inch (3 mm), cut slabs, and cover all visible elements of the Parthenon, including the cardboard base. Once every part is covered in chocolate, attach the roof to the foundation and secure it with two thin dowels.

4. Using a clay extruder fitted with a ½ cm square die, create squared ropes of ivory modeling chocolate and set them aside for use later.

5. Press ivory modeling chocolate into a 4½-inch (11 cm) wide triangular silicone heirloom mold to create pediments for the triangular sides of the roof. Trim them to size and brush them lightly first with cocoa powder then with super pearl dust to add depth and sheen. Set them aside.

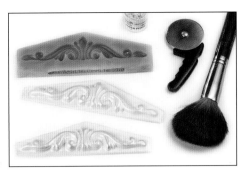

6. Roll ivory modeling chocolate to ¼-inch (6 mm) thickness and cut into ¾-inch (19 mm) squares to serve as *metopes* (decorative stone panels that line the *frieze* above the columns). With white chocolate, pipe Greek letters and symbols. Once set, brush them with cocoa powder and super pearl dust. Set them aside.

7. To make the columns, melt 24 oz of white and 12 oz of dark chocolate. Thin them out with enough vegetable oil to achieve a thin but clingy consistency. Set the dark chocolate and a small portion of the white aside for later. Pour the white chocolate to a 3-inch depth in a drinking cup. Begin dipping approximately 40 Pirouettes® (only 32 are needed for the cake, but some may break with handling so making some extra is a good idea) into the cup of white chocolate, touching each column to the bottom before pulling it out. Pause after dipping to allow the excess chocolate to run off into the cup. Frequently (every three dips or so) replenish the chocolate in the cup to maintain a 3-inch depth so that the level of the chocolate on the columns maintains uniformity.

8. Scrape each column once against the lip of the cup to remove any remaining excess chocolate, then place it scraped-side down on a sheet pan lined with parchment paper.

9. Once all the columns have been dipped in white chocolate, set them briefly in the refrigerator to set.

10. Empty the remaining white chocolate in the cup back into the main supply. Add a teaspoon or enough dark chocolate to the white to create a slightly darker ivory tone. Proceed with the same dipping method, this time maintaining a shallower cup depth of 2¼ inches. Place the columns the same side down on parchment paper, maintaining a flat back to later adhere to the sides of the cake. Allow the twice-dipped columns to cool completely.

11. Empty the remaining ivory chocolate back into the main supply and darken it with a tablespoon of dark chocolate or enough to achieve an amber color. Pour the amber chocolate into the cup to a shallower depth of 1½ inches and proceed to dip each of the columns in the same manner as above.

12. Repeat the process a fourth time, using a milk chocolate tone and a cup depth of ¾ inch. Once all the rods are dipped and set, trim the tops with a paring knife so that each column can fit snugly in the space between the cardboard base and overhanging lip of the roof. Eyeball or measure 32 spots for the columns around the periphery of the Parthenon, making sure they are equidistant from one another. Dab a small amount of white piping chocolate on the flat backs of the columns to act as glue. Adhere them one by one to the monument's walls.

13. Measure and cut the square modeling chocolate ropes prepared earlier to equal the lengths of the four sides of the structure. With white chocolate, affix the ropes just underneath the rows of columns to create *stylobate* (the stone rim that runs around the base of the columns), framing them from below.

14. With white and medium chocolate, pipe overlapping layers at the top of each column to convey a decadent interpretation of the ionic capital. With dark piping chocolate, pipe a ruffled base around the bottom of each column.

15. Decorate the frieze with the *metopes* made earlier, spacing them slightly apart. Pipe a vertical line pattern between each *metope* to render *triglyphs*. Lay the remainder of the squared rope atop the *metopes* to delineate the *frieze*. Affix the pediments to the triangular spaces on the short sides of the roof. Pipe three different tones of melted chocolate onto the roof as decoration. Pipe a ruffled border over any seams or flaws to conceal the handiwork. Insert dowels into the center of the roof to support the cake mountain and lighthouse above. Add the second mountain of cake and insert enough dowels to support the weight of a gingerbread lighthouse.

For tutorials on gingerbread houses, check out the Wicked Goodies website at www.wickedgoodies.com

Bonus Chapter:
Pearl Cascade Design

The pearl patterns cascading from the tops and bottoms of each tier on this cake are buttercream interpretations of the festive Mexican *papel picado* banners, a decorative scissor and paper craft. The 28 shades of buttercream pearls that appear on the cake are derived from nine basic hues.

145

1. Mix and match buttercream colors prior to use to yield the most balanced palette. Make ¼ cup of each of the above concentrated hues, reserving at least 2 cups of vanilla buttercream. Each of the six dot cascades consists of five gradients of color. Each group of five is achieved by mixing hues with different ratios of vanilla buttercream to achieve gradually softer tones.

2. In this example, the colors range from dark turquoise to light green. Number the paper cones 1 to 5 for easy reference.

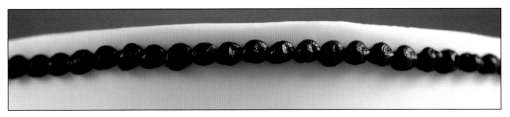

3. Start with one straight row of pearls in the darkest color out of the five. Begin one-quarter inch below the top of each tier, (beginning at the very top may cause the frosting to sag as the cake softens to room temperature).

4. In the next lightest shade, nest clusters of three in the crevices of the above row. Skip one out of every three.

5. Nest clusters of twos in the next lightest shade and so on.

6. Like laying a pyramid of bricks, each row guides the placement of the next.

7. One additional row of single pearls spaced away from the body of the trim creates a drip effect.

8. Fill in the spaces between with streams of pearls in gradations of both color and size to evoke a piñata streamer effect. Here is a good place to improvise if you are so inclined.

9. Proceed in the same manner on the rest of the cake tiers, juxtaposing complimentary colors as opposed to following a rainbow order.

Here is a template of the design. Photocopy it and slip it under parchment paper. Then practice.

To learn how to make the colorful modeling chocolate carnations on this cake, see pg. 65

Buttercream Recipes

Vanilla Buttercream

This is a recipe for American-style buttercream, which means that no cooking or eggs are involved. It works beautifully as a frosting for wedding cakes and special occasion cakes because it holds up to stacking and is resistant to cracking.

The butter in this buttercream, when refrigerator cold, keeps cakes solid, intact, and easy to maneuver. At room temperature, it is soft and easy to cut through. The use of a food processor eliminates any trace of lumps, which makes ultra-fine finishes (with no drag marks) possible and detailed piping (with no clogged tips) easier to pull off. The texture is silky smooth and the real vanilla extract yields an intoxicating flavor and aroma. The only downside of this recipe is that it involves dirtying two machines, but I think it's worth it. This is an adaptation of a recipe that I learned working at a bakery named "Cake."

Items Needed

- Electric mixer, preferably the standing variety, with paddle attachment (whisk is okay)
- Food processor
- Rubber spatula
- 1 lb 6 oz (2¾ cups) unsalted butter, softened to room temperature but not melted or overly soft
- 1.7 lb (6 cups) confectioners' sugar
- ½ cup (118 ml) whole milk at room temperature
- ¾ teaspoon pure vanilla extract

1. **Allow the butter** to come to room temperature (3–4 hours).

2. **Using a paddle attachment,** mix the butter on low speed for 1 minute until it is slightly whipped.

3. **With the mixer running on the lowest speed,** begin adding the confectioners' sugar ½ cup at a time.

4. **Once two-thirds of the confectioners' sugar** has been incorporated, add the milk and vanilla.

5. **Promptly** add the remainder of the confectioners' sugar.

6. **Stop mixing** when the ingredients are roughly blended. The frosting may be very lumpy and broken-looking at this stage. That is okay.

7. Using a rubber spatula, transfer the frosting into a food processor fitted with a standard chopping blade. Process the buttercream for 2–4 minutes, or until it is perfectly smooth and runs fluidly in the machine.

8. Using the rubber spatula, scrape the sides of the bowl then process the frosting for 30 seconds more. There should be no more visible lumps when the frosting is done.

    Store vanilla buttercream in a sealed container or a bowl covered in plastic wrap. It is best held at room temperature out of sunlight. Depending on the freshness of the butter, vanilla buttercream can last for 10 days or more at room temperature. If held in an airtight container in the refrigerator, it can last for up to three months. If held in an airtight container in the freezer, it can last for up to six months.

    To color buttercream, add liquid food coloring, one drop at a time, stirring thoroughly until the desired hue is achieved.

Chocolate Buttercream

For the chocolate version of this buttercream recipe, use the same technique for making vanilla buttercream but apply the following formula:

Items Needed

- 1 lb 6 oz (2¾ cups) unsalted butter, softened to room temp (but not melted or overly soft)
- 1.4 lb (5 cups) confectioners' sugar
- 4 oz good quality (not Hershey's) unsweetened cocoa powder
- ½ cup (118 ml) whole milk
- ¾ teaspoon pure vanilla extract
- Pinch of table salt

Frosting Technique

1. To frost a wedding or special occasion cake with this type of buttercream, first add a thin crumb coat to the outside of the cake to seal in the crumbs. Set the cake in the refrigerator to firm up.

2. Once the crumb coat is firm, add a thicker ½-inch coating of buttercream. Use an offset spatula to distribute the frosting evenly over the surface of the cake, then use a bench scraper to smooth the sides.

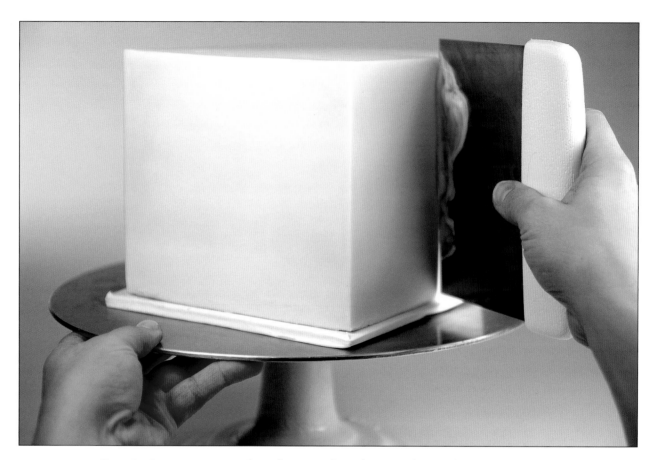

3. Allow the frosting to set in the refrigerator for at least one hour. Then scrape the sides of the cake with the blade of a bench scraper to smooth the finish. Using an offset spatula, fill in any gaps or imperfect edges with more buttercream, then allow the cake to harden in the refrigerator before scraping the sides again. Repeat this process until the sides of the cake are perfectly smooth and the corners are square.

    A cake frosted in all-butter buttercream should be held in the refrigerator until it is ready to go on display. Allow the cake to come to room temperature so that the buttercream is soft when served.

Round Cake Serving Chart

Diameter	Height	Servings	Circumference
5 inches	4 inches	8	16 inches
6 inches	4 inches	10	19 inches
7 inches	4 inches	15	22 inches
8 inches	4 inches	20	26 inches
9 inches	4 inches	25	29 inches
10 inches	4 inches	30	32 inches
11 inches	4 inches	40	35 inches
12 inches	4 inches	50	38 inches
13 inches	4 inches	60	41 inches
14 inches	4 inches	70	44 inches
15 inches	4 inches	80	48 inches
16 inches	4 inches	90	51 inches
17 inches	4 inches	100	54 inches
18 inches	4 inches	110	57 inches

Square Cake Serving Chart

Diameter	Height	Servings	Circumference
4 x 4	4 inches	8	16 inches
5 x 5	4 inches	12	20 inches
6 x 6	4 inches	15	24 inches
7 x 7	4 inches	22	28 inches
8 x 8	4 inches	30	32 inches
9 x 9	4 inches	40	36 inches
10 x 10	4 inches	50	40 inches
11 x 11	4 inches	60	44 inches
12 x 12	4 inches	72	48 inches
13 x 13	4 inches	80	52 inches
14 x 14	4 inches	95	56 inches
15 x 15	4 inches	110	60 inches
16 x 16	4 inches	125	64 inches
17 x 17	4 inches	137	68 inches
18 x 18	4 inches	150	72 inches

Rectangular Cake Serving Chart

Diameter	Height	Shape	Servings	Circumference
8 x 12	4 inches	1/4 sheet	25	40 inches
12 x 16	4 inches	1/2 sheet	50	56 inches
16 x 24	4 inches	full sheet	100	80 inches

More cakes decorated in modeling chocolate by *Wicked Goodies*

Armadillo cake

Artist's Palette cake

Dios de los Muertos cake

Firetruck cake

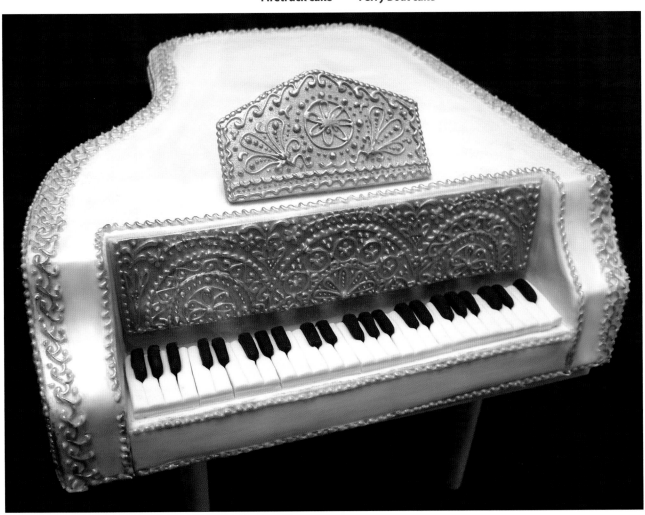

Ferry Boat cake

Grand Piano cake

Even more cakes decorated in modeling chocolate by *Wicked Goodies*

Jack Daniels cake

Aircraft Carrier cake

Paintball cake

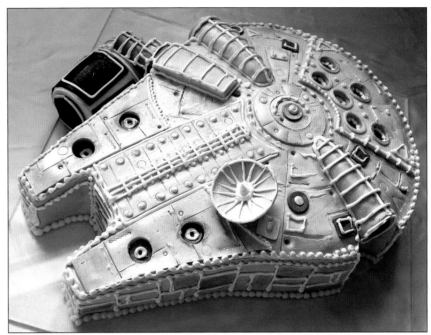

Millenium Falcon cake

Letterman's Jacket cake

Leaning Tower of Pisa cake

Glossary

Bittersweet chocolate. Has the lowest percentage of sugar and therefore the edgiest flavor. It is often denoted by the percentage of cocoa materials present, which can range anywhere from 35 to 100 percent. The higher the percentage of cocoa, the lower the percentage of sugar, and therefore the more bitter the taste. Bittersweet chocolate, rich in both color and taste, makes an excellent, not-too-sweet modeling chocolate.

Bleeding. When a finished cake is exposed to temperature extremes, condensation may form on its surface, causing dark colors to bleed or streak. To avoid this problem, allow a frozen cake to defrost fully in the refrigerator before decorating it.

Buttercream. A whipped cake frosting made primarily from sugar and butter. I use American-style buttercream, which contains butter, confectioners' sugar, milk, and vanilla extract.

Cake drum. A sturdy, foil-covered cake base made from heavy cardboard that is designed to withstand the weight of large cakes.

Cell formers. Typically made from plastic or silicone, these are used to help fondant, modeling chocolate, or gumpaste decorations hold a particular curvature or shape. The silicone version is more costly but works best for forming modeling chocolate flowers.

Clay extruder. A small cylindrical device with a plunger that forces clay (or in this case modeling chocolate) through a small die to produce uniform shapes that are rope or string-like.

Cocoa butter. The yellowy, natural fat of the cocoa bean that is responsible for the melting/hardening properties of chocolate. It is an extremely complex and unique lipid whose long molecules, when heated and cooled correctly, form the tight bonds that give tempered chocolate its shine and snap. No other natural fat performs quite like it.

Compound chocolate. The technical term for imitation chocolate that is made with some or all hydrogenated fats in place of real cocoa butter.

Cornstarch. A fine white hydroscopic powder often used to coat candies, modeling chocolate, marshmallows, and other confectioneries to prevent them from sticking together.

Corn syrup or light corn syrup. The optimal sugar syrup for making confectionery because of its pliability and resistance to crystallization. In the U.S., it is cheap and readily available. Outside the U.S., it is harder to find and may be prohibitively expensive. Unfortunately its manufacturing process cannot be replicated in an ordinary home kitchen. When it comes to modeling chocolate, corn syrup may be substituted for liquid glucose.

Craft utility knife. Better known by the brand name, X-Acto, this type of handheld knife has small replaceable blades and is typically used for fine craft projects. In this context, it is used to cut modeling chocolate.

Crumb coat. A thin frosted layer of buttercream that is applied to the outside of the cake and allowed to harden. The purpose of the crumb coat is to lock loose crumbs down so that they don't infiltrate the finish coat.

Dowels. Wooden rods that are used in cake construction mostly as infrastructure to prevent stacked cakes from slipping or collapsing under the weight of themselves.

Elephant skin. Term used to describe fondant when its surface grows dry and crusty to the extent that it is no longer workable, at which point it will crack if handled, causing it to look fissured and weathered like an elephant's skin. This problem does not occur with modeling chocolate.

Finish coat. A thick layer of buttercream that is applied over the crumb coat and is smoothed for a fine, seamless finish.

Foam shaping mat. A piece of soft foam that provides a flexible surface for shaping and thinning flowers and decorations made from fondant, gumpaste, or modeling chocolate.

Fondant. (iced or rolled) A sweet dough-like confection often made from glucose + gelatin or confectionery sugar + marshmallows, which is commonly used to make edible decorations or to cover cakes.

Inlay effect. In the context of modeling chocolate it involves layering a sheet of rolled modeling chocolate with a pattern or design also made of modeling chocolate, then rolling them between sheets of parchment paper until they bind into one seamless design such as leopard or zebra print.

Linear marble effect. The technique of repeatedly twisting and folding ropes of two or more colors of modeling chocolate, then rolling them out to yield a marblized sheet whose striations run in one direction.

Liquid glucose. A dense sugar syrup used in food and confectionery that is often replaced by its cheaper counterpart, corn syrup. It is too complex to produce in the average home kitchen but it is obtainable worldwide. It tends to be costly.

Luster dust. Also referred to as pearl dust, gold dust, disco dust, or white sparkle, it comes in different colors and is used to create shimmery, gilded, or glittery effects on cake decorations.

Modeling chocolate. Also known as plastic chocolate, chocolate leather, or candy clay, it is a soft, pliable confection made from chocolate and sugar syrup. It can be used in place of fondant for nearly every existing decorating technique. Although it requires more patience and finesse than fondant, it is far superior in flavor and versatility.

Sweet and creamy, it melts on the tongue like soft, candy bar nougat. Slow to dry, it is the ideal substance for modeling shapes and figurines.

Milk chocolate. Dark chocolate with a milk product added. Although it can be used for modeling chocolate, its softness is not optimal for ease of handing or stability.

Parchment paper. A cellulose-based releasing paper for baked goods and confectionery. When used to line baking pans, it prevents food from sticking to metal or paper, greatly extending the life of the pan. It may also be used as a working surface for modeling chocolate. Quilon-coated, full sheet parchment is the best and most versatile, as it is durable and can be trimmed to any size.

Parchment paper cone. A triangle of parchment paper that has been formed into a cone, which can be filled with decorating substances like melted chocolate, royal icing, or buttercream, then closed off and used like an pen for writing and piping.

Pasta machine. A small machine that rolls dough or modeling chocolate into small sheets and can be adjusted to yield different thicknesses.

Piping chocolate. Melted chocolate combined with enough vegetable oil to yield a pourable consistency that is ideal for piping and writing on cakes. *See* "12 Cake Writing Tips" on the Wicked Goodies website for the formula and instructions.

Plunger cutters. A type of cutter with a spring-loaded release mechanism that enables a cake decorator to produce and maneuver cut-out shapes more efficiently.

Rolled modeling chocolate. The term for modeling chocolate that has been rolled by hand or through a machine until thin. Rolled modeling chocolate is an excellent medium for rendering flower petals, leaves, ribbons, bows, and fabric effects. It can be used to wrap cakes as an upscale alternative to fondant. It can be marbled or patterned with any design.

Roller cutter. More commonly called a pizza cutter, this tool is used in cake decorating to trim fondant, modeling chocolate, and gumpaste.

Seizing. When liquid, steam, or too much heat is introduced to chocolate, it will clump into a mass. Seized chocolate can usually be saved with the addition of a warm fat like butter or cream. To avoid seized chocolate, make sure the bowl and all utensils are complete dry before use. Also be sure to avoid overheating the chocolate.

Semisweet chocolate or dark chocolate. Typically intended for baking purposes and commonly found in chip form. It is essentially dark chocolate that has been sweetened at a 1:2 ratio of sugar to cocoa. It works well for modeling chocolate.

Sheeter. A bakery machine that rolls dough, fondant, or modeling chocolate into sheets. Either automated or lever controlled, most sheeters can be adjusted to yield different thicknesses.

Sweet chocolate. A term used only by U.S. standards to represent a lower quality sweetened chocolate containing no more than 15 percent real chocolate liquor. It works fine for modeling chocolate but has a diminished quality of taste.

Swirled marble effect. The technique of repeatedly twisting and folding ropes of two or more colors of modeling chocolate, forming them into coils, then rolling them out to yield a marblized sheet whose striations swirl.

Tempering. A more advanced pastry technique that entails heating and cooling chocolate to specific temperatures in order to optimize the strength, shine, and snap of a product. It is not necessary to temper chocolate when making modeling chocolate.

Titanium dioxide. A natural white dye derived from titanium. The food grade version, which comes in a powder or liquid form, is used to whiten products like modeling chocolate.

Topper. The term for an ornament that sits atop a cake. Popular toppers include a spray of fresh flowers or sugar flowers, a pile of fruit, or a pair of ceramic figurines.

Turntable. A round revolving platform made from wood, metal, or ceramic that is used in cake production and decoration.

Veiner. A one- or two-sided mold, usually made of silicone, which when pressed against a piece of modeling chocolate, fondant, or gumpaste, forms the impression of veins on leaves or petals.

White chocolate. A confection composed of sugar, milk and fat(s). True white chocolate contains cocoa butter, which lends an ivory tint to the hue. The quality and performance of white modeling chocolate is greatly affected by the brand of white chocolate used.

Index

Resources

Online Equipment Resources in the U.S.

Chef Rubber, Nevada. Wide selection of silicone molds, transfer sheets, showpiece supplies, and ingredients like gum arabic and isomalt.

Ateco, New York. The best brand of stainless steel cutters, piping tips, piping bag supplies, turntables, spatulas, and hand tools.

Fat Daddio's, Washington. An excellent West Coast resource for high quality, factory-direct baking pans and equipment.

Global Sugar Art, New York. Almost everything you'd need to get started baking and cake decorating.

Sugarcraft, Ohio. This site is not the easiest to navigate, but it has an incredibly wide selection of items for all forms of confectionery.

Wilton, Illinois. Sells a popular line of decorating supplies, how-to books, and cake decorating courses that are widely available in craft stores throughout the U.S. and Canada.

CK Products, Indiana. Manufactures and distributes an array of instructional manuals and candy-making supplies.

Online Equipment Resources in the U.K.

Cake Decorating Company, Nottingham. Abundant range of cake decorating tools including make-your-own silicone molds, cake push-pops, and harder to find brands. The retail shop also offers classes on topics such as cake decorating, sugarveil, and airbrushing techniques.

Design a Cake, Washington. Equipment, tools, consumables, molds, and veiners galore.

Squire's Kitchen, Farnham. Tools for baking, wedding cake design, chocolate making, and sugarcraft, with a retail shop that offers classes for all skill levels.

Windsor Cake Craft, Warrington. Kitchenware, consumables, decorating supplies, which are also available at their retail shop.

Recommended Books

Baking Illustrated by the Cooks Illustrated Magazine Editors, America's Test Kitchen; First edition (2004). Recipes that were perfected in a test kitchen with detailed analysis of the ingredients and how they best perform together.

Baking with Julia: Savor the Joys of Baking with America's Best Bakers by Dorie Greenspan, William Morrow Cookbooks; First edition (1996). I bake from this book quite often. It is wonderful.

The Cake Bible by Rose Levy Beranbaum, William Morrow Cookbooks; Eighth edition (1988). The best resource for tried-and-true cake recipes, with baking conversions for most scenarios.

Martha Stewart's Baking Handbook by Martha Stewart, Clarkson Potter; First Edition (2005). Includes clever baking tips and recipes that I've implemented both at home and in commercial bakeries.

On Food and Cooking: The Science and Lore of the Kitchen by Harold McGee, Scribner; Revised updated edition (2004). The ultimate reference book on food science. Explains how ingredients perform on a molecular level and how they've been sourced and manufactured historically. My #1 reference book.

Professional Baking by Wayne Gisslen Wiley; Fifth edition (2008). This book is comprehensive and full of color photos and recipes. It's more of a food science, food textbook kind of book.

About the Author

I am **Kristen Coniaris,** the creator of Wicked Goodies. I hold a Professional Chef's Degree from the Cambridge School of Culinary Arts and have 17 years of experience in the food industry specializing in bakery management, product development and cake artistry. As of 2013, I have engineered over one thousand custom wedding cakes, three award-winning gingerbread houses, and a gigantic rooster cake covered in modeling chocolate for TLC's reality show, *Fabulous Cakes.*

 www.facebook.com/WickedGoodies

 www.pinterest.com/mywickedgoodies

 www.twitter.com/WickedGoodies

 www.youtube.com/user/myWickedGoodies

Check out the Wicked Goodies website

www.WickedGoodies.com for free tutorials and videos on the topic of baking and cake design such as:

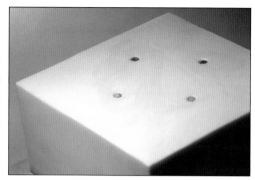

How to use Wooden Dowels in Stacked Cakes

How to Taper Cake Tiers

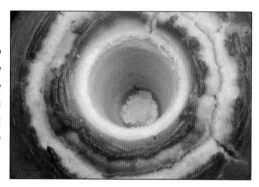

How to Bake a Cake with a Heating Core

12 Cake Writing Tips

How to Make a Motorcycle Cake

How to Make Chocolate Glaze

How to Sculpt with PVC, Rice Treats, and Modeling Chocolate

How to Make a Topsy Turvy Cake

How to Fill Cakes

How to Make a Boat Cake

How to Make a Car Cake

What to do with Left-over Cake

How to Make a Hamburger Cake

How to Make an Owl Cake

How to Make Zoo Animal Cupcakes

Which Cake Pans to Buy

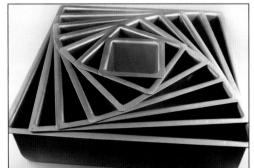

Award-winning Gingerbread House Designs by Wicked Goodies

Santa's Workshop Gingerbread House

This 3½ foot wide, 3½ foot tall gingerbread house interpretation of Santa's workshop won first place at the 2012 Boston Christmas Festival.

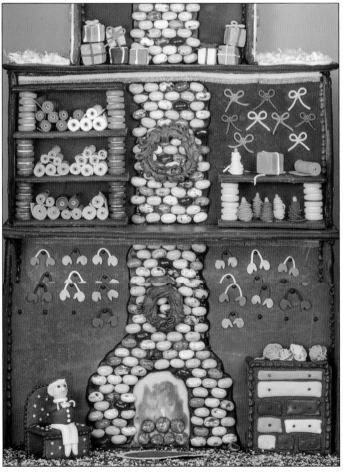

Alice in Wonderland Gingerbread House

This 4 foot x 4 foot x 2½ foot gingerbread house interpretation of Alice in Wonderland won second place in the 2009 Gingerbread City Competition in Del Mar, CA. It is made of gingerbread, royal icing, gum paste, and candy.

Wonka Factory Gingerbread House

This 4 foot x 4 foot x 3½ foot gingerbread house interpretation of Willy Wonka's Chocolate Factory won second place in the 2010 Gingerbread City Competition in Del Mar, CA. It is made of gum paste, gum, candy, 100 pounds of gingerbread dough, and 150 pounds of royal icing.

Gingerbread House Design

A photo guide to baking, decorating, and assembling homemade gingerbread houses.